Every new professional needs a mentor, and beginning teachers benefit from the kind veteran teacher down the hall. Johnson, Kay, and Stuart give us just that: the helpful voices of wisdom and experience. They welcome us into the best professional conversations with each other and leaders like Penny Kittle and Thomas Newkirk.

Their advice is sound. John Hattie's research provides the underpinning, and the authors show how to set up and run classrooms truly responsive to students.

Their advice is so practical! They offer multiple techniques, such as many ways to quote students in your classroom and how to leverage the grading load.

Best and most rare of all, their advice models learning. Pointing us toward online sources like the *Cult of Pedagogy* and the *National Writing Project*, they share how they have evolved as teachers, even creating language (buzzwordified!) and crackling the prose with concepts like literacy evangelism.

If I can't teach down the hall from these three, this book is the next best thing.

Gretchen Bernabei
Teacher, Consultant, and Author

Johnson, Kay, and Stuart are asking great questions that will lead to life-giving, sustainable ELA teaching and learning. The practices they describe in their own rooms leap off the page because of their authenticity and dynamic delivery. We need more books like this by teachers who love students and have a passion for building our profession by inviting others into their classroom practices in ways that allow educators and students to flourish.

Jonathan Eckert
Author of *Leading Together: Teachers and Administrators Improving Student Outcomes*

Reading this book is like having three experienced mentors give you all the answers on the ELA teacher test! If you are looking for teaching moves, engaging assignments, and resources to cultivate a true learning community, get ready to be inspired. Truly a gift for early-career teachers looking for ideas, midcareer teachers who need a boost, and veteran teachers who are ready to be refreshed. Johnson, Kay, and Stuart shine a united voice of optimism on teaching in today's classrooms.

Carol Pelletier Radford
Author of *Teaching With Light: Ten Lessons for Finding Wisdom, Balance, and Inspiration*; *Mentoring in Action: Guiding, Sharing, and Reflecting With Novice Teachers*; and *The First Years Matter: Becoming an Effective Teacher*

Matthew Johnson, Matthew Kay, and Dave Stuart have hit a home run with their new book *Answers to Your Biggest Questions About Teaching Middle and High School ELA*. Their practical suggestions for cultivating classroom community and instructional ideas are valuable for not only the novice educator, but the seasoned one as well. I found myself thinking of ways I could use their suggestions in my own university literacy teaching! This trio has crafted a text that ELA folks will want to keep on their desk so they can quickly reference these easy-to-implement classroom ideas.

Rebecca Harper
Author of *Write Now and Write On, Grades 6–12*

Johnson, Kay, and Stuart have written a book to help navigate the burning questions early-career teachers long to understand. From ways to build a community of learners to motivational instruction to feedback that works for students and teachers alike, these inspirational teachers share what it takes to craft a career for the long haul.

Andy Schoenborn
Coauthor of *Creating Confident Writers: For High School, College, and Life*

Matthew Johnson, Matthew R. Kay's, and Dave Stuart Jr. book *Answers to Your Biggest Questions About Teaching Middle and High School ELA* is an excellent resource for teachers looking to implement best practices in classrooms immediately. New teachers will find inspiration and resources as they plan and implement ELA curriculum in both the middle and high school English classroom. Johnson, Kay, and Stuart detail common challenges in the ELA classroom and provide practical strategies and solutions for the new *and* experienced teacher.

Theresa Walter
English Teacher, Nationally Board Certified Teacher (NBCT)

Johnson, Kay, and Stuart have written a book that would seem to answer every question I asked myself in the last year. They not only answer the questions with immediately useful suggestions one could apply to their class on the spot, but they also offer responses that are grounded as much in research as they are in optimism and joy. Though they began this book with beginning teachers in mind, they realized, as we all have in the last few years, that we are all new teachers who need the wisdom and practical strategies these three generous teachers offer us to do our job. My wife and I, because of the overwhelming demands of our personal and professional lives in the last few years, started getting one of those meal kits delivered a couple of days a week. I was reminded of those kits and how much they have helped us be a bit more healthy and balanced as I read *Answers to Your Biggest Questions*, which Johnson, Kay, and Stuart would no doubt appreciate, for in their introduction, they say we should use and think of their book "as a serious cook uses a new cookbook." This book will help any teacher cook up lessons that are as consistently delicious as they are healthy—both for students and their teachers.

Jim Burke
English Teacher, Middle College High School and
Author of The Common Core Companion series

Under the weight of overwhelming expectations and intimidating systems of power, ELA teachers can ease their heavy load by hitching up with Johnson, Kay, and Stuart. From each of their unique teacher zones, the authors provide do-able options—rather than do-it-all presumptions—to help teachers strengthen learning communities with empathy, engagement, and equity. *Answers to Your Biggest Questions* offers a hope, clarity, and practicality needed to make this work lighter and brighter.

Erica Lee Beaton
Author of *The Good Enough Teacher*

In *Answers to Your Biggest Questions About Teaching Middle and High School ELA,* three great yet distinctive teachers have put together a book that hits that rare balance of big-picture inspiration and down-home practical advice. Matthew Johnson, Matthew Kay, and Dave Stuart make their teaching visible in a way that will work both for early-career teachers and (as Matthew writes) "anyone who wants to be new." Most importantly, they keep it real: real questions, real dilemmas, and real responses full of options and activities. ELA teachers will want to keep this one close at hand.

Elyse Eidman-Aadahl
Executive Director, National Writing Project

Answers to Your Biggest Questions About Teaching Middle and High School ELA pools together the extensive classroom experience of Matthew Johnson, Matthew R. Kay, and Dave Stuart Jr. There are moments from their classrooms, their best strategies, and their favorite resources, all contextualized by powerful mental framing to help teachers of English language arts narrow their focus, work more efficiently, and make sure our valuable minutes with students move them forward as learners. Open up the book to any page, and you'll find something you can use now—for example, my students have already considered the authors' meaningful list of five reasons to read. This book will invite you to imagine better possibilities for you and your students.

Sarah M. Zerwin
High School Language Arts Teacher, Instructional Coach, and Author of
Point-Less: An English Teacher's Guide to More Meaningful Grading

Johnson, Kay, and Stuart are three of the best writers, sharpest thinkers, and kindest humans in our profession. These are the mentors every teacher should have! Written in engaging, heartfelt prose, *Answers to Your Biggest Questions About Teaching Middle and High School ELA* rings with teacher truths on every page. This book is a gift not only to new teachers but to all of us seeking a renewed commitment to our life's work.

Jennifer Fletcher
Author of *Teaching Arguments* (2015), *Teaching Literature Rhetorically* (2018),
and *Writing Rhetorically* (2021)

As a former high school English teacher, this book is the book I wish I had. As a high school principal, this is the book I will make sure is in the hands of every English and Language Arts teacher in my school. It is a thoughtful, practical and kind text that will help teachers build a student-centered English classroom with a culture of reading and writing that will help students years after they leave its walls.

Chris Lehmann
Founding Principal—Science Leadership Academy
Coauthor of *Building School 2.0*

ANSWERS *to Your* BIGGEST QUESTIONS *About*

TEACHING MIDDLE & HIGH SCHOOL ELA

FIVE to
THRIVE

ANSWERS to Your
BIGGEST QUESTIONS About

TEACHING MIDDLE & HIGH SCHOOL ELA

Matthew Johnson
Matthew R. Kay
Dave Stuart Jr.

CORWIN

For information:

Corwin
A SAGE Company
2455 Teller Road
Thousand Oaks, California 91320
(800) 233-9936
www.corwin.com

SAGE Publications Ltd.
1 Oliver's Yard
55 City Road
London EC1Y 1SP
United Kingdom

SAGE Publications India Pvt. Ltd.
B 1/I 1 Mohan Cooperative
Industrial Area
Mathura Road, New Delhi 110 044
India

SAGE Publications
Asia-Pacific Pte. Ltd.
18 Cross Street #10-10/11/12
China Square Central
Singapore 048423

President: Mike Soules
Vice President and Editorial Director:
  Monica Eckman
Executive Editor: Tori Mello Bachman
Content Development Editor: Sharon Wu
Editorial Assistant: Nancy Chung
Project Editor: Amy Schroller
Copy Editor: Amy Hanquist Harris
Typesetter: Integra
Proofreader: Lawrence W. Baker
Indexer: Maria Sosnowski
Cover Designer: Gail Buschman
Marketing Manager:
  Margaret O'Connor

Printed in the United States of America

Library of Congress Cataloging-in-Publication Data

Names: Johnson, Matthew M., author. | Kay, Matthew R., 1983- author. | Stuart, David R., Jr., author.
Title: Answers to your biggest questions about teaching middle and high school ELA / Matthew Johnson, Matthew R. Kay, Dave Stuart Jr.
Other titles: Answers to your biggest questions about teaching middle and high school English Language Arts
Description: First Edition. | Thousand Oaks, California : Corwin, [2022] | Series: Corwin Literacy
Identifiers: LCCN 2022001215 (print) | LCCN 2022001216 (ebook) | ISBN 9781071858042 (Paperback) | ISBN 9781071880647 (ePub) | ISBN 9781071880654 (ePub) | ISBN 9781071880661 (Adobe PDF)
Subjects: LCSH: Language arts (Middle school) | Language arts (Secondary) | English language--Study and teaching (Middle school) | English language--Study and teaching (Secondary) | Effective teaching. | Teachers--In-service training.
Classification: LCC LB1631 .J643 2022 (print) | LCC LB1631 (ebook) | DDC 428.0071/2--dc23/eng/20220310
LC record available at https://lccn.loc.gov/2022001215
LC ebook record available at https://lccn.loc.gov/2022001216

This book is printed on acid-free paper.

22 23 24 25 26 10 9 8 7 6 5 4 3 2 1

CONTENTS

3   HOW CAN I ENSURE THAT MY FEEDBACK AND ASSESSMENT ARE BOTH AS EFFICIENT, EFFECTIVE, AND EQUITABLE AS POSSIBLE?   60

4   WHAT DOES STRONG ELA INSTRUCTION LOOK LIKE?   90

5   HOW CAN I KEEP DOING THIS FOR MY WHOLE CAREER?   116

ACKNOWLEDGMENTS

First, we'd like to thank our families. Cat, Cait, and Crystal, and our children all put up with a lot while we three were putting this book together. We love you!

Then to those amazing teachers we've worked with—Ken, Judith, Jessika, Tracy, David, Celinda, Doug, Erica, Painter, Jim, Zac, Larissa, Amal, and many others. Thank you for inspiring us.

Also a sincere thanks to all of those administrators who have supported us: Rebecca, Carmie, Debbie, Jeremy, Ron, Jen, and Chris.

And we've been so fortunate to work with incredible editors on this project. Tori Bachman, Lisa Luedeke, Sharon Wu, and Nancy Chung—your steady hand and vision helped to make this book what it is.

And lastly, thank you to all of our colleagues near and far who are reading this book. As an educator, your time is one of your most valuable assets, and we are so honored and thankful that you entrusted some with us.

PUBLISHER'S ACKNOWLEDGMENTS

Lydia Bowden
Assistant Principal, Gwinnett County Public Schools

Andy Schoenborn
English Teacher, Clare Public Schools

Theresa Walter
English Teacher, Great Neck Public Schools

ABOUT THE AUTHORS

Matthew Johnson spent the first half of his career teaching middle school English language arts and social studies in Oregon and California, and he currently teaches high school American Literature, African American literature, composition, and film at a public magnet high school in Ann Arbor, Michigan. He is also a longtime track coach and the author of *Flash Feedback: Responding to Student Writing Better and Faster — Without Burning Out* (2020), a book about how to turn responding to student work from one of the most time-consuming, difficult, and often unsustainable parts of teaching into one of the most joyful and replenishing things we do as teachers.

Matthew R. Kay teaches kids at Science Leadership Academy in Philadelphia, Pennsylvania. He currently teaches 9th and 10th graders English, and has taught elective courses in drama, critical race theory, and African American literature. He's also been an athletic director and is currently both the head varsity basketball coach and an assistant football coach. He is the author of *Not Light, But Fire: How to Lead Meaningful Race Conversations in the Classroom* (2018). Finally, he's the executive director of the Philly Slam League, a non-profit that shows Philly-area young people the power of their voices through weekly spoken word competitions.

Dave Stuart Jr. teaches in a small town just north of Grand Rapids, Michigan. He's taught grades six through twelve during his career, in both English and social studies. He wrote about his comprehensive approach to simplifying teaching in *These 6 Things: How to Focus Your Teaching on What Matters Most* (2018), and he publishes weekly articles for teachers at DaveStuartJr.com/newsletter and weekly videos at DaveStuartJr.com/YT.

The time in which we write these words, autumn of 2021, is hardly an optimistic one for many educators. After 18+ months of pandemic teaching, educators across the country face immense workloads, social-emotional challenges, and burnout that they could have never imagined two years ago, while their schools and districts strain under teacher shortages and gladiatorial school board meetings.

Not much glimmer, right? And yet, we are deeply optimistic. True, there is a lot that is worrisome—some things we don't yet know, and much we can't control. But there is also so much that is exciting: new voices offering fresh solutions to old problems, new ideas and discoveries lighting the way to a better education system for all.

There is also so much that we do know, and thus can better control, now. We have more information each day about how students learn, what motivates them, and how and when they form community. And we also have more tools with each passing school year to be more efficient—to do a better job of communicating with and guiding students and responding to and assessing student work in less time, allowing us more balance in our own lives. This increased communal knowledge allows us greater control of these things in our classes, even when there are other things outside our classrooms that we wish we could control more.

This book is about the exciting developments and the things we know now and can control. It is about those new voices and ideas that hold the promise of helping make the lives of millions of students better. It is also about getting more efficient with the things that matter so that we can live more balanced and sustainable teaching lives. It is about growing more effective in our practice so we can better help students in this, and any future, hours of need, finding a way to thrive when even just surviving can feel like an unreasonable goal.

In short, this is an optimistic book about optimistic things because there is so much that is working and can work, and those are the things we need to move from this foggy and dark moment we are in to a better, brighter tomorrow.

WHO IS THIS BOOK FOR?

We originally wrote this book with an audience of brand new teachers in mind, basing it upon the things we wish we'd known in our first year or two with students. But as we wrote, the book slowly evolved into a book that also highlights the ways in which *all* teachers can refine their practice and the ways *all* teachers can balance the job, given the daily stresses so many teachers face.

Just a bit before finishing the final manuscript, Matt Kay said, "I think this book is for anyone who wants to be new." Matt Johnson and Dave Stuart nodded vigorously in their Zoom call—*yes*. That's just right. In the same way that each new fall offers an opportunity to be new and to finally do it right this year, this book looks at how—regardless of whether you are just beginning that first year or embarking on year 35 or 40 of a long and storied career—we can seek to be new and better and balanced in the week, unit, or school year to come.

This book is broken into five big questions—questions whose answers are fundamental to finding your footing or improving your groove as a classroom professional:

- How do I build a brave and supportive reading and writing community?

- How do I cultivate motivation in an ELA classroom?

- How do I ensure that my feedback and assessment are both as efficient, effective, and equitable as possible?

- What does strong ELA instruction look like?

- How can I keep doing this for my whole career?

In these chapters, we offer some of the things we've learned over our careers. Most of them are not new or unique to us. Instead, we showcase the moments, lessons, books, ideas, materials, and mentors that have helped us do what you are doing now with this book in your hands: striving to be better tomorrow than we are today.

WHO WE ARE

We are three midcareer, actively practicing high school English language arts teachers. We're united in our heart's desire to see teachers, and especially early-career teachers, gain their footing and flourish in this work long term. Here's a bit more about each of us individually.

Matthew Johnson spent the first half of his career teaching middle school English language arts and social studies in Oregon and California, and he currently teaches high school American literature, African American literature, composition, and film at a public magnet high school in Ann Arbor, Michigan. He is also a longtime track coach and the author of *Flash Feedback: Responding to Student Writing Better and Faster—Without Burning Out* (2020), a book about how to turn responding to student work from one of the most time-consuming, difficult, and often unsustainable parts of teaching into one of the most joyful and replenishing things we do as teachers.

Matthew R. Kay teaches kids at Science Leadership Academy in Philadelphia, Pennsylvania. He currently teaches ninth- and tenth-grade English, and he has taught elective courses in drama, critical race theory, and African American literature. He's also been an athletic director and is currently both the head varsity basketball coach and an assistant football coach. He is the author of *Not Light, but Fire: How to Lead Meaningful Race Conversations in the Classroom* (2018). Finally, he's the executive director of the Philly Slam League, a nonprofit that shows Philly-area young people the power of their voices through weekly spoken-word competitions.

Dave Stuart Jr. teaches in a small town just north of Grand Rapids, Michigan. He's taught both English and social studies to Grades 6–12 during his career. He wrote about his comprehensive approach to simplifying teaching in *These 6 Things: How to Focus Your Teaching on What Matters Most* (2018), and he publishes weekly articles for teachers at www.DaveStuartJr.com/newsletter and weekly videos at www.DaveStuartJr.com/YT.

HOW TO USE THIS BOOK

In this book, you will find the teaching moves, assignments, and resources that we use in our classes to cultivate community; teach, respond to, and assess students; and build student identities as young readers, writers, and scholars. It also has the voices and reminders we turn to when we feel our candles burn low, want our students to get a little bit more metacognitive, or need to figure out how to reach that one student who seemingly can't lift his head up, no matter what we try.

As your starting point, we'd like you to think about this book as something akin to the lessons left on the copy machine, those little slices of teaching that you notice as you walk down the hall, or that colleague from next door who offers a new perspective that helps you to make that next lesson or unit just a little bit better. We also (at the risk of mixing metaphors) encourage you to use this book the way that a serious cook uses a new cookbook. Take what is useful, make it your own and improve upon it, follow the leads that you find interesting, and ultimately use it all to make something so new and nourishing that even those who didn't know that they were hungry will make space for an extra helping.

Best to you, colleague.
MJ, MK, and DS

chapter ONE

HOW DO I BUILD A BRAVE AND SUPPORTIVE READING AND WRITING COMMUNITY?

Each ELA class is a unique writing and reading community. Sometimes, when jumping from one distinctive section to another, the contrast can be invigorating; other times, when we're frustrated at not recreating the magic in third hour that we felt in second hour, it can feel hard. But it is what it is: Our classes will develop their own norms, routines, and feelings whether we want them to or not. What *is* in our control is the kind of moves and postures that we can use to help to cultivate the types of communities we're after, using what and how we say and do on purpose. That's what this chapter centers on.

What we're after is the active construction of class cultures that are courageous, curious, and collaborative; social places where students listen to each other, finding themselves both pushed and secure, challenged and inspired. We want a classroom where students measure their strengths and successes based on their own growth.

The sense of community we're after is opposed to classrooms that are transactional, fearful, or overly competitive, where students broadcast without listening or stifle themselves due to fear of judgment. In classrooms like this, students measure their strengths and successes against their peers' talents—a road to disenchantment.

This chapter will focus on how to build a reading and writing community that is closer to the former than the latter, which is not an easy task, given that the world outside our classrooms often favors the individual over the collective

(Hammond, 2014, p. 17), and that ethos of individuality often walks in with students on the first day of school.

So how do we build the kind of reading and writing communities that help our students to be their best selves? To get to the roots, we'll answer the following questions in Chapter 1:

☐ **What community-building exercises work best in a reading and writing classroom?**

☐ **How can I get students to work with each other seriously and thoughtfully?**

☐ **How can student sharing of work develop community?**

☐ **How can I get students to listen to everyone in the classroom (including one another, teachers, and texts)?**

☐ **What role does listening on the part of the teacher play in building a strong community?**

☐ **How can I dislodge negative narratives students carry about their reading and writing identities?**

☐ **What are the best practices around student independent reading?**

☐ **What role does debate play in building a strong community?**

☐ **What role does celebration play in building community in the classroom?**

What Community-Building Exercises Work Best in a Reading and Writing Classroom?

Before getting into some dedicated community-building exercises, it is important to acknowledge that we should consider community building as the work of our curriculum choices and pedagogical moves throughout the entire school year. True community is not built with a couple of initial exercises. But with that said, here are a few of the isolated exercises that help build community in our ELA classes.

Community-Building Exercises to Start the Year

- **Minefield**. On day one of the school year, Matt Kay often takes a bunch of printer paper and spreads it on the floor. He then asks for two volunteers. One closes their eyes, and the other one has to guide them through the "minefield" (the papers can also represent puddles or whatever hazards you find appropriate), using only their voice. When the blindfolded student steps on a paper, everyone in the class says "Bang!" or "Splash!" Matt volunteers to go last as a student guides him through. The kids have a lot of fun. After finishing, the class recaps. "If this activity is a metaphor for how you'll need to communicate with each other this year, what do you think the lesson would be?" (The guide role teaches us to explain ourselves clearly, knowing that our colleagues can't always see what we see. The walker role teaches how important it is to communicate when we don't understand an instruction and so on.) This activity cuts through the noise on a day of "be-good" rules and syllabi reading, and it hints that this will be an ELA class that will get students on their feet a bit.

- **Story of My Name.** We have all experienced classroom moments where teachers mispronounce a whole pile of student names on the first day. This is common enough that it may not seem like a big deal, yet when a teacher regularly mispronounces a student's name, it can have meaningful negative effects on the student (Rice, 2017), given a name's often deep connections to family, culture, and one's own sense of identity. Further, messing up a student's name in your first act as the steward of a new class does not leave a good first impression. In Matt Johnson's class, students introduce their name on the first day by writing and then telling the class the "story of their name," which is whatever they want it to be. This activity allows the teacher to hear the name first before saying it, helps the teacher and classmates know a bit more about the student, and establishes a theme of the importance of learning the stories of one's classmates.

- **First-Day Index Cards**. Dave Stuart asks students to begin their year in his classroom by writing their preferred name on one side of an index card and describing the person they'd like to become on the other side. It's this second part—the aspirational side of the card—that Dave uses to launch a community focused on the pursuit of long-term flourishing via the mastery of reading, writing, speaking, and knowledge building. Students write and share statements such as the following:

- I want to be generous.
- I'd like to be a dependable friend.
- I hope I can be a kid my parents can be proud of.

- **Speed Dating.** Sometime in the first week, students in Matt Kay's class do a speed-dating activity. The kids split into two groups and stand in concentric circles, facing a partner of the opposite group. Matt asks a low-stakes question, such as "What's a guilty pleasure song you love to listen to?" Each student answers it, and then the inner group rotates. The questions eventually move to slightly more serious questions like "What is something you are excited about this year?" but nothing that requires significant vulnerability. Besides being a getting-to-know-you activity, it prepares students for some of the one-on-one conversational structures that they'll be using.

To read more about this exercise, check out Dave's blog post on the idea; the QR code in the margin will take you there.

Example Speed-Dating Questions

1. What is your favorite food?
2. What is a "guilty pleasure" song that you like?
3. What's your most embarrassing moment? (They normally love this one; just remind them that it doesn't have to be "serious" embarrassment—more like tripping in front of your crush.)
4. Tell a story about a horrid/awesome teacher you've had in the past.
5. What were you proudest of yourself for last year?

> True community is not built with a couple of initial exercises.

Community-Building Exercises to Use Throughout the Year

- **House Talk: Burn 5, Good News, and High-Grade Compliments.** In *Not Light, But Fire* (2018), Matt Kay describes three activities meant to help students feel more secure participating in what he calls "House Talk." (Remember when you were a kid, and your parents said something like, "Don't repeat what you just heard. That stays in the house." Essentially, house talk is making space for those conversations that flow naturally in a supportive classroom "family.") These three activities can be modified to match your preference or what your students find meaningful. Good News and High-Grade Compliments were inspired by Matt Kay's brilliant former colleague Zac Chase's classroom.

  - *Burn 5.* Speak informally with students before every class period. Check in about popular TV shows, athletic contests, school dances—anything that lets us speak with them about something other than our formal curriculum.
  - *Good News.* Start the week giving kids a chance to share something good from their lives. Modification: Let them share "highs and lows."

- *High-Grade Compliments.* Whenever necessary and appropriate, invite students to walk over to classmates and publicly share what they appreciate about each other. Modification: When your day is full, shorten this to sharing brief public "shout-outs" in whole-class time.

- **What Makes Us Special**. As Dave Stuart progresses through the year, he loves to emphasize to each of his class periods what makes them special, particularly through keeping running jokes or lines with each hour. For example, in this past year, Dave told his first hour all the time that they were the next best thing to a cup of coffee; his second hour developed a special reverence for one of the YouTube teachers that Dave used for instructional clips during remote learning; and in his third hour, class members refer to their classmate who was elected the homecoming prince as "His Highness" on a regular basis. These small, good-natured through lines help each class to feel like something mundane (e.g., third hour) is something special because, after all, it is! There has never been a third hour exactly like the one you teach this year.

- **Two-Way Feedback.** Feedback in the classroom can generally be compared to a river, where response flows downstream from teacher to student. In our classes, though, we strive to approach feedback in the way of a whirlpool, where both teachers and students regularly provide and receive important information. Getting out of the monologue feedback mode and engaging in a discussion that never ceases can initially be scary for both parties—it can be nerve-wracking to listen to and truly hear from someone who knows us, after all—but it can ultimately empower both parties and strengthen their connections to each other. For the students, this quietly teaches them that their voices matter and trains them to be more reflective and metacognitive; for the teachers, it informs them with real-time data about how the class is going, allowing them to be more reflective and metacognitive as well. Specifics about how to best provide and receive feedback both ways will be discussed in depth in Chapter 3, but the simple move of making space for everyone to speak and listen will go a long way toward creating a positive and powerful classroom community.

Notes

How Can I Get Students to Work With Each Other Seriously and Thoughtfully?

Many of us, when we were kids, groaned internally (or out loud!) when our teachers assigned another group project. Many of your current students do the same. "Here we go again. Mrs. _____ is going to pair me up with _____, and I'm going to end up doing all the work." Or "I'm going to be the one who goes to the teacher to say that _____ is being a jerk." Or "Now I'm going to have to watch five *boring* group presentations with kids standing in line to read off a PowerPoint that we all can read for ourselves just fine." It's easy to dismiss these and so many other concerns as laziness or self-centeredness or any other attribute commonly ascribed to modern, "whiny" students.

Yet in the real world, so many of these concerns are valid. When there is a single "group grade," it *is* hard to incentivize some students to not tap out, forcing their more grade-conscious classmates to do most of the work. It is equally hard to convince "school-y" kids to let their less traditionally talented classmates contribute meaningfully with the specter of a bad "group grade" hanging over their heads. And group projects often *are* socially awkward. When the students have issues with a group's dynamic, they have to either "snitch" to their teacher or take matters into their own hands. And lastly, traditional stand-in-a-line-and-read-off-a-sheet/ slidedeck group presentations *are* boring and seem to take forever for every member of the class to say (or usually read) their "part."

Group projects are no picnic for teachers either. Yes, it might feel awesome to see a 32-project grading load morph into an eight-project breeze. But try figuring out who did what or who understands what part of the story or who needs a bit more help with a specific writing skill. Try explaining the "lessons learned in self-advocacy" to irate parents whose kid's GPA was just threatened by a low "group grade."

Add all of this together, and we should probably listen to group-project critics of all ages. They often have a point. However, collaboration is deeply important; students need to work and play together if we want our class communities and the students themselves to reach their full potential. What we have to understand to solve this dilemma is that collaboration does not inherently mean "group projects." It means that we give students plenty of opportunities to discuss texts, to respond to each other's writing, and to practice presentations—all as part of the regular flow of class—and that we don't always attach this collaboration to some sort of group grade. In fact, we've found that decoupling collaboration from "group projects" is often more effective at getting them to work together than both the hard sell and any punitive grading techniques we used to employ to try to get kids to buy into working together in those projects.

Some of the ways to achieve this integration of group work into the wider work of class include the following:

- **Divide the class into small learning communities** that meet regularly to discuss the reading. This can be before quizzes, after read-alouds, as projects are assigned, and so on. Matt Kay has had success having students record their sessions and upload them as assignments that are "graded" only for general participation.

- **Encourage students to thoughtfully cite each other's contributions** to both small-group and large-group conversations in their analytical writing. Begin by asking students to take notes during class discussions in which they jot down strong points and ideas made by both their classmates and themselves. Then, follow this with encouraging students to analyze one to three quotes from classmates in their analytical essays and grow from there.

- Similarly, **encourage students to use each other's ideas and stories as inspiration** for their creative and analytical writing projects. We should design projects that ask students to pool their creative ideas.

- **Reframe peer review.** Instead of peer review being a once-a-semester major editing session, try having more regular, smaller "conversations" where students turn and discuss some element of their work. These small, lower-stress moments of micro peer review will normalize peer interaction, making the bigger peer-to-peer conversations better (see Chapter 3), and you will get more high-quality feedback into the classroom.

Here is what Matt Johnson tells his classes before the first time they take notes on a class discussion:

> In most classes, students take notes on lectures. But these days, lecture slides are often the one thing from class that is readily available on class websites. Meanwhile, other parts of class, such as the insights of one's classmates (which can be equally insightful as any lecture), only exist for a few moments before they get dislodged by another set of ideas or dissolve into the ether. That is why in this class I want you to have your notebook open to capture those brilliant discussion ideas from your classmates so that you can build on them in papers and projects later.

 Equity and Access

All collaboration needs to be designed with students' access in mind. For instance, students who have to work after school might not be able to meet up with their groupmates. Students might not have certain tech tools (a nice smartphone with a camera, a printer, etc.) and should not be put in a position to be embarrassed about it, to spend money to get it, or to have the lack of it hurt a group grade.

 We should design projects that ask students to pool their creative ideas.

How Can Student Sharing of Work Develop Community?

Teenagers are risk-takers. This, understandably, drives us bonkers as their classroom teachers and makes mentoring them . . . well . . . challenging at times. But as ELA teachers, we are uniquely positioned to benefit from this fraught stage of brain development. Two things help us out. First, we constantly ask students to create. Second, most people are terrified—across various levels—about public speaking. This means that, for a significant portion of our students, publicly sharing work (that they care about, at least) has the potential to get their heart rates thumping, their palms sweaty, their voices caught in their throats. It's risky to put themselves "out there," and it is viscerally thrilling when they succeed.

Once exposed to this particular thrill, many students spend their academic careers chasing it by joining drama clubs, poetry teams, student governments, and the like. Others just get an opportunity to be proud of themselves, which can be rare in some students' school journeys. In both cases, students get the chance to support each other, strengthening the individual bonds that support a classwide sense of community.

Sharing work *well* in the classroom can be difficult, though, because even for risk-taking adolescents, the natural fear of public speaking can stand in the way of them sharing on a regular basis. If we desire classes where sharing is more of a norm than an exception, we need to be more strategic than simply asking every once and a while *Does anyone have a piece they want to share?* and hoping for the best. We can increase their likelihood to contribute by doing the following to help students feel as though they can be successful in sharing their work:

- Give them time to practice before they present.

- Clarify the purpose of any sharing moment. If students are sharing so that we might all celebrate them, make that clear. If this is *not* the time for substantive feedback, make that clear. Students should have a general idea of whether to gird themselves for critiques or not when sharing something that means a lot to them.

- We can create a culture of celebration by uplifting *encouragement* as a core value and publicly celebrating kids who are the most encouraging. These super encouragers should also be rewarded with private pull-asides and emails home, copying colleagues (see Figure 1.1). It's good to be known as the teacher who loves when kids are effusive with support.

- Ensure that the mechanisms for praise have been routinized. Students feel oddly vulnerable when showing appreciation for a classmate's efforts. This vulnerability can cause that sincerely felt compliment to never actually leave a kid's mouth. It gets easier when there are dedicated "shout-out" sessions after sharing activities, some sentence starters to kick-start praise, or even praise-centered guided notes to make sure that kids don't forget what they liked after an extensive presentation.

Figure 1.1 Example Encouragement Letter to Colleagues

Team ___,

I just wanted to give a public shout-outs to _____ for being a wonderful citizen of SLA, especially in regard to her support and encouragement of classmates.

_____, your buddy _____ really gave you a lot of credit in his reflection for pushing him to finish this dystopian novel benchmark, which ended up being so important for his grade (and probably just helping him to feel proud and more confident). I really appreciate how you support not just ___ but everyone else in _____. Your positive energy has meant so much to everyone this crazy school year. It feels like you are being very intentional about bringing joy to your classes, and it has made all the difference.

I'm so happy that I've gotten the chance to teach you.

Mr. Kay

- Look for different ways for students to share. Matt Johnson's students often do cascading quick-shares where they share a favorite sentence or example of a skill, one after another, so that there is a certain anonymity in the pace. He also starts his year with blank walls in his classroom—a sort of anti-Instagram look—so that he can fill the walls with shared student words and ideas as the year progresses (see his "What We Should Read" wall later in Chapter 1).

Sentence Starters for Kick-Starting Praise

- I really appreciate _____.
- I want to give _____ a shout-out for _____.
- _____ really impressed me with _____.
- _____ really inspired me with _____.

Notes

How Can I Get Students to Listen to Everyone in the Classroom (Including One Another, Teachers, and Texts)?

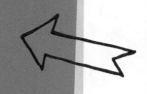

In the K–12 classroom, kids' underdeveloped listening skills are usually described as poor behavior. Teachers often try to manage this misbehavior by scolding, shaming, or handing out low participation points or some other disciplinary action, and while guilt and fear might get kids to make eye contact with classmates and zip their lips shut for now, neither inspires students to authentically listen to each other.

Listening authentically is effortful, after all. It takes significant bandwidth for students—and, frankly, their teachers—to tune out distractions and lock in on any speaker's ideas for even the shortest amount of time. At best, guilt and fear just give kids enough inspiration to convincingly fake the effort.

Instead, the biggest selling point for listening to others is not to "be well behaved" or "be nice." It is to understand that classmates' contributions have value. If these contributions aren't collected, analyzed, debated, and appreciated, a student is missing out on something important.

WAYS TO ENCOURAGE LISTENING IN THE ELA CLASSROOM

- Offer discussion prompts inspired by specific student contributions to class discussions and/or writing. And let students know which student contributions have led to these prompts!

- Pull back the veil to show the class how their discussion prompts have been inspired by specific student contributions to class discussions and/or writing.

- After small-group or one-on-one conversations, encourage students to share what they found most interesting about their partners' contributions.

- "Sit with" students' comments a bit longer to model active listening. "Sitting with" is like "wait time," except *after* a student speaks. Don't be in a rush to weigh in or to call on the next student. Make a bit of a show of chewing on the idea that was just shared. Then, if practical, consider reprompting the class in a reaction to what the student shared. "Lana said _____. I think it's a great point! But if that's true, then how does that impact _____?"

- Try to have a clearly more patient tone when addressing students' poor listening skills versus when addressing misbehavior. Instead of an exasperated and annoyed shout of "One voice!" maybe we could just remind them how awesome their classmate's contribution is. "Hold on, did you hear this? _____ is saying _____! You don't want to miss this!"

Create lessons and assignments that make listening easy and fun, not hard and dull. In the vein of a Golden Shovel poem, which is a poetic form created by Terrance Hayes where you embed a Gwendolyn Brooks poem into your own original poem, Matt Johnson has his students share a poem with another student and then write their own original poem that embeds elements of their partner's poems. Much like a fast-paced soccer game can make working out fun and a just-right novel can inspire thousands of pages of impromptu literary analysis online, creating the right listening fun can make the often difficult task of hearing one's classmates a joyful ease.

Notes

What Role Does Listening on the Part of the Teacher Play in Building a Strong Community?

We should, of course, model the listening behaviors we want from our students. We can do this by citing students' comments generously and analyzing their ideas patiently. We can ask thoughtful follow-up questions. We can sit with student responses and repeat their thoughts and ideas back to them days or weeks later. This is a good start; however, if a strong classroom community is the goal, it requires more than this academic listening.

We also need to model the rich listening that is rooted in care. There are many ways to do this. Enthusiastically engage students' minor tangents. Be patient when introducing assignments, even when the same question is asked four times. Slip in a personal question ("How was your basketball game? Did you have a good weekend?") when you see students in the hallway or the lunchroom.

But there is one more way that listening can help teachers build a strong classroom community. We can (1) acknowledge the uneven power dynamic between us and our students and (2) show evidence that, through listening, we have worked to make this dynamic more equitable.

WAYS TO USE LISTENING TO BUILD A STRONG CLASSROOM COMMUNITY

- **Don't wait for the end of the year to do a course evaluation.** At a minimum, ask students to offer feedback on your course after a quarter or preferably after each unit. Further, student feedback doesn't have to come via larger course evaluations. Teachers can create quick Google Forms (Figure 1.2) where students can give flash feedback to teachers too. We also advise that teachers act upon these so that students can see they were heard and address any relevant observations openly.

- When teaching a unit, **make it clear when you adjust based on previous students' feedback.** For instance, every year when introducing a graphic novel project, Matt Kay tells students how the first version was suggested by students.

- **Give an opportunity for students to recommend texts** that they discover during independent reading units. Have a *Should I teach this? Why or why not? If yes, what kind of projects could I do with it?* section on any end-of-book evaluation.

- When the suggested books are used in any way, **give discovery credit to past or current students** who brought it to your attention.

In Dave's class, he's quick to **acknowledge and celebrate when students bring up an evidence-based complaint.** For example, after a unit assessment Dave overheard a pair of students complaining about a particular question on the assessment, arguing with one another that their answers had been correct. Dave asked them to tell him more, and they matter-of-factly shared evidence for why their answers were legitimate. Dave praised them for this work and said that he agreed; he then received their permission to share the conversation with the whole class.

Whatever the type of assessments a teacher uses, **ask students to self-assess and share those self-assessments with you first.** Chapter 3 goes deeper into the whys and hows of student self-assessment, but few things level the dynamic between student and teacher more than having scores/grades evolve through a conversation, not through something that is "given" by the teacher.

Figure 1.2 An example of a Flash Feedback form for students to fill out

Friday Check-In

Here is your Friday check-in. Please turn it in by the end of the day, if possible. Thanks, everyone! You rock!

How have the first three weeks of class been?

Long answer text

What is working for you so far in class? What should I definitely keep or do more of?

Long answer text

What could I do better or what isn't working? Is there anything you are confused about? And do you have any worries or concerns about the class that I should know about?

Long answer text

How Can I Dislodge Negative Narratives Students Carry About Their Reading and Writing Identities?

COMMUNITY

A simple truth: We have no control over the reading and writing lives of the students in our care before they arrive in our classrooms. We don't know what frustrations they have had with writing, what narratives they have assumed about themselves as writers, or what comments they have absorbed from previous teachers and classmates. We do, however, have control over what types of writing and reading kids do while they're in our classrooms—and we often have the power to undo some of the negative instruction and experiences kids have endured.

Many educators think that before students write meaningful stuff, they must learn the basics: English grammar and mechanics, spelling and vocabulary, and narrative story arcs and analytical five-paragraph structures. This approach is tempting in its simplicity. After all, if students never commit to capitalizing the first word of their sentences, how will their future résumés ever pass muster? Isn't it the "soft bigotry of low expectations," as George W. Bush would say (eMediaMillWorks, 2000), to let students write stories or poems when they lack the discipline to indent their paragraphs? Surely they must crawl before they can walk, walk before they can run, and run before they attempt to write a dystopian novel.

Of course, too many students take one look at this approach and internalize that they are hopeless walkers in a world of effortless sprinters. Year after year, the curriculum has teased them with, "Once you get this down, you'll be able to . . . , " and year after year, they don't get to do anything cool. Or at the end of the year, they get to do *one* cool thing. Matt Kay will always remember leading a creative writing class midyear—right out of undergrad—and asking his new students what they'd written so far that year:

"Nothing."

"*Why?*"

A kid held up a grammar workbook and said, "We been doing these."

Matt was staggered. "It's February!" No stories. No poems. No plays. No songs. No memoir vignettes. Nothing but preparation. He imagined an athlete working tirelessly on free throws yet never playing games—not even playing pickup at the park with friends. What's the point? After a while, she wouldn't feel like a basketball player. She'd feel like a free throw shooter. The kids in this classroom didn't feel like writers with indentation issues. They felt like apprentice indenters taking an indenting class because the "real world" really cared about indentation.

When it comes to students not viewing themselves as writers, it's not just teachers telling kids directly or indirectly that they are bad writers, even though that certainly happens. It's that the writing process has often become so hyperfragmented and so rigidly sequential that kids rarely get to the cool part. And even if they get to the appropriate mastery, they often have to wait for their classmates who are on their own timetables.

Similar things are true when it comes to reading identities and instruction. Matt Johnson finds nearly every year that his students identify more by their Lexile or test scores than their favorite books when he asks them about their reading lives. Further, like writing, reading instruction far too often exchanges meaningful interactions with texts for an endless parade of strategies that once mastered simply beget two more additional strategies, like a boring hydra that really likes annotation.

Of course, annotation is a deeply important skill—one that all three of us adore in our personal lives and teaching practice—and students do need to know about grammar and story arcs. But if we want to turn around deeply internalized negative narratives that concern reading and writing and help our students to truly assume the stance of "I am a writer/reader," we need to do a lot more. Here are some ways to aid in this transformation:

- **Don't let any particular skill focus keep a student from creating.** There may be a space for the old-school, nonnegotiable approach to teaching where you'll ask students to resubmit until they sort out certain mistakes. But the timing matters. Always let students brainstorm, get feedback on their ideas, and write outlines and drafts, and never let a creative process get derailed in order to attend to a skill deficit.

- A simple formula holds us accountable for giving kids multiple reliable chances to see themselves as writers: **Whatever they are reading, they are also writing.** If our students are reading plays, they should be writing plays. If they are reading memoirs, they should be writing memoir vignettes. Whatever the students are reading and discussing is a mentor text, and it is our job to mine each one for techniques they can critique, replicate, and/or build upon.

- **Put these projects front and center.** Announce them early and mention them often as you progress through the texts so that students can see the connection between what they are reading and what they will be soon producing.

- **Ask about a student's reading and writing history and use that information to inform your approach.** At the beginning of the year, you can ask students to write you a letter about their reading/writing/academic lives (see Figure 1.3 and the online companion). It is important that these letters are open-ended and not graded (if they are graded) on anything but completion so that students feel allowed and encouraged to tell the important parts of their history in these areas and tell them honestly. The information gathered from these lessons is often like a cheat sheet that can be used in the sabotaging of their negative reading and writing identities and the cultivation of more positive identities to take their place

- **Give students time and space to discuss their reading lives.** Have your students choose some of their own reading (more on independent reading later in Chapter 1), find ways for them discuss their reading lives with classmates, ask for book recommendations from them, and even have them bring in models of favorite ledes or characterization from their favorite books to augment the mentor texts the teacher brings. These rich discussions and displays of their reading lives will feed the reading identities of those who already read and model what a rich, joyful reading life looks like for those who do not identify as readers.

Figure 1.3 Example of Introductory Letter Assignment

To begin our year together, I would like you to write me a letter or some other variety of bio. The goal of this letter/bio is to introduce (or reintroduce) yourself to me, and as such, the topics you cover and the approach you take are fully up to you. It will be assessed purely on you giving it your best, which means there is no need to stress about spelling, grammar, sentence structure, and so on. We will get to those things, but I'm not worried about them right now. Also, feel free to write it however you want. It can be in prose or poetry, a story or a stream-of-consciousness rant. Just sit down at a keyboard and be you, and I'm excited to hear what you have to say!

Some potential topics you can discuss follow.

Who You Are

- What are your interests and goals? What impact would you like to make on the world? What dreams do you have?
- What do you do outside of school? What do you do to relax? What passions do you pursue and/or art do you create?
- What is your story?
- What would you like others to say about who you are?
- What are your pet peeves?

Your Story as a Reader

- What is your story as a reader?
- How often do you read? What do you like to read? What are your all-time favorite books/comics/poems/short stories/websites/other things one can read?
- What do you *not* like to read?

Your Story as a Writer

- What is your story as a writer?
- How do you feel about writing? What are the successes, struggles, twists, and turns you've had?
- What do you like and not like to write?

Your Story as a Student

- What is your story as a student?
- What are you hoping to get out of this year? What are you hoping we don't do in this class?
- What type of teaching works best for you? What doesn't work? And what have your most successful teachers done to make their classes work for you?

Equity and Access

Make sure that the material students read represents a variety of cultures, backgrounds, and experiences. Similarly, make sure that students get a chance to write about a variety of cultures, backgrounds, and experiences.

What Are the Best Practices Around Student Independent Reading?

In 2019, the National Council of Teachers of English (NCTE), one of the oldest and most respected language arts teacher organizations, published a position statement, arguing that choice or independent reading had the "most significant impact on student success in reading." Citing research by Richard Allington (2014), NCTE issued this statement:

> The more one reads, the better one reads. The more one reads, the more knowledge of words and language one acquires. The more one reads, the more fluent one becomes as a reader. The more one reads, the easier it becomes to sustain the mental effort necessary to comprehend complex texts. The more one reads, the more one learns about the people and happenings of our world. This increased volume of reading is essential. (2019, para. 3)

This is a bold claim, but it also makes sense that the best way to get better at something is to do it a lot. It also makes sense that if we want our students to identify as serious readers, we need to get more serious about this "most significant" part of our reading instruction toolbox. In short, we need to put our time and our planning where the research is and commit class and planning time to independent reading.

We hear what you're probably thinking: **Given my curriculum, school, and district requirements, how do I make space for independent reading too?** There is no button that one can push to suddenly make room for independent reading in our curriculum. Something will have to go, but if we are thinking about it in terms of priorities, what is more important than finding a way for the students to read more? According to NCTE and a host of reading specialists and researchers, not much, if anything.

When Matt J. first grew more serious about independent reading, he struggled with letting go of content and spent several years giving voice to the importance of independent reading while not allocating much time or thought to it. The results of this were as middling as one might expect from a halfway commitment, but when he finally got serious about allocating class time to increased volume—50 minutes every week—and regular discussion of students' reading lives, those middling results suddenly metamorphosed into one of the biggest jumps in skills and engagement that his classroom has ever seen.

How Much Independent Reading/Writing Time Should Students Have?

Longtime reading instruction researcher Dr. Richard Allington (2002) recommends a roughly 50/50 ratio of reading/writing to other "stuff," such as discussions, group work, teaching strategies, and more (p. 742). For an easy way to figure out how much independent reading is appropriate for your class, you can add up all of the reading and writing happening in your class during a given unit and see how close it gets to that golden reading/writing-to-stuff ratio.

When one commits to independent reading, it isn't as simple as pointing the students in the direction of good books and saying go. Even though it is powerful, it isn't a panacea, and there are plenty of missteps that can impede its effectiveness. Here are some best practices that can make the return on that investment as big as possible:

- **Have a meaningful discussion about why independent reading is a part of class time.** Over the years, we have had a few students challenge us to explain why independent reading is a part of class time. Discussing as a class the value of independent reading both *during and outside of class* can motivate those who don't see its value and those who are lukewarm readers or decidedly anti-reading to commit to and more meaningfully engage with independent reading. We share the following "Why Read?" reasons with our students:

Reason #1: Reading is a powerful stress reducer.
The Earl E. Bakken Center for Spirituality and Healing at the University of Minnesota (n.d.) shared the following:

> Reading can be a wonderful (and healthy) escape from the stress of everyday life. Simply by opening a book, you allow yourself to be invited into a literary world that distracts you from your daily stressors. Reading can even relax your body by lowering your heart rate and easing the tension in your muscles. A 2009 study at the University of Sussex found that reading can reduce stress by up to 68%. It works better and faster than other relaxation methods, such as listening to music or drinking a hot cup of tea. This is because your mind is invited into a literary world that is free from the stressors that plague your daily life. (para. 2)

Reason #2: Reading is good for your long-term health.
A Yale University School of Public Health study found that book readers live on average two years longer than non-book readers (Flood, 2016), and reading can help to both ward off and slow cognitive decline and dementia (John, 2013). A potential argument for why the invisible act of reading has these tangible impacts comes from neuropsychologist Robert Wilson, whose research suggests that "exercising your brain by taking part in activities [like reading] across a person's lifetime, from childhood through old age, is important for brain health in old age" (Castillo, 2013, para. 3).

Reason #3: Reading makes you a better you.
Reading has been found to make us more empathetic, improve our social cognition, and make us stronger leaders because it offers insights into others and practice at developing theories of mind that allow us to better understand the people around us (Hammond, 2019).

Reason #4: Reading helps us to process difficult times.
James Baldwin once said, "You think your pain and your heartbreak are unprecedented in the history of the world, but then you read. It was books that taught me that the things that tormented me most were the very things that connected me with all the people who were alive, who had ever been alive" (Goodreads, n.d.a). And Maya Angelou said, "When I look back, I am so impressed again with the life-giving power of literature. If I were a young person today, trying to gain a sense of myself in the world, I would do that again by reading, just as I did when I was young" (Goodreads, n.d.b). Reading can help us to feel connected and unique, which are both potent tools for navigating hard times.

Reason #5: Reading is fun.
The most important reason to read is that reading is fun! Getting to travel somewhere else as someone else is a type of magic that simply doesn't exist anywhere else.

- **Resist grading independent reading.** We have used reading logs, projects, and other graded work over the years in an effort to keep students on task. Unfortunately, these extrinsic motivators often transform independent reading from something we do to grow as students and people to the students checking off boxes to get a grade. When we stopped using logs and having independent reading projects, the focus shifted to students reading for themselves, and our classroom libraries suddenly got a lot emptier.

- **Provide students with true choice during independent reading.** It's tempting to ask students to choose books from a curated list of grade-appropriate or course-related books. Ideally, this knocks down two birds with one book, as it gets them "choice" reading while also accomplishing curricular objectives. In practice, though, these lists often don't accomplish either goal particularly well. Any curated list of books is going to cut off many of the most high-interest texts for students while also not granting them the rich experience that can come with reading something along with others in the class.

- **Don't micromanage the level of reading.** Many schools put a lot of emphasis on things like Lexile scores or reading levels, so it can feel natural to require certain levels of reading or vocabulary for independent reading. In our experience, however, doing this can cause more harm than good because forcing students out of their comfort zone or shaming them for a pick that is "below grade level" can push them further away from increasing their amount of reading. And when it comes to doing far less reading in books with higher Lexiles/reading levels or far more reading in books with somewhat lower Lexiles/reading levels, if we are talking about growth, increased quantity will win every time.

- **Rely on reading conferences for assessment.** While we don't grade independent reading or writing, we do have reading conferences where we talk to students about the ups, downs, questions, and answers that have come from their reading. Conferences are far more accurate and less draconian than other types of accountability measures such as book logs or parent/guardian signatures that are easily faked and that can diminish student motivation by associating choice reading with checking off boxes (Nguyen, 2021). Such conferences are also a wonderful tool for getting to the bottom of what makes reluctant readers unenthusiastic and offering book recommendations for indecisive readers.

- **Independent reading generally works best when it's social.** One of the biggest impediments to independent reading is that some students, having potentially never been given free rein to read what they want, don't know how to find the right book for themselves. The key to helping with this is to have lots of book talks where the teacher or (even better) fellow students preview and celebrate books that they or others have loved. (See Figure 1.4.)

Figure 1.5 "What Should We Read" Board

In Matt J.'s classes, students start the year by giving short book recommendations, which Matt puts into Google slides that are then easily printed at the one secret (shhhh!) color printer at his school and posted in class as ongoing recommendations for others.

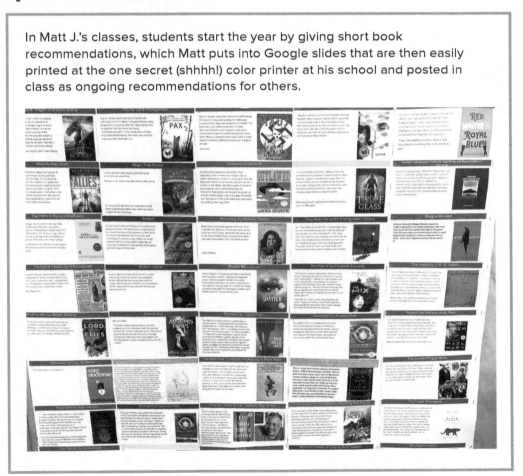

Great Resources

- Kelly Gallagher. (2009). *Readicide: How Schools Are Killing Reading and What You Can Do About It*. Stenhouse.

- Berit Gordon. (2017). *No More Fake Reading: Merging the Classics With Independent Reading to Create Joyful, Lifelong Readers*. Corwin.

- Penny Kittle. (2012). *Book Love: Developing Depth, Stamina, and Passion in Adolescent Readers*. Heinemann.

- Donalyn Miller. (2009). *The Book Whisperer*. Jossey-Bass.

Notes

What Role Does Debate Play in Building a Strong Community?

When ELA teachers encounter "maximally controversial" issues in our curriculum—defined by Jonathan Zimmerman and Emily Robertson as a conflict where parties are "fairly competent" with respect to the issue, have a significant emotional investment, and are discussing matters of public concern (2017, p. 49)—the most risk tolerant among us address the issue via classroom debates. While there are variations on the exact procedure for such debates, in the general flow, students are invited to first stake out a position. We might say, "Stand on one side if you believe _____; stand on the other if you believe _____." Or after giving a prompt, we might say something like, "Raise your hand if you think _____. Good. Now raise your hand if you think _____. Excellent." Then, we move to some version of, "Can I have one volunteer from each side?" The kids share, and boom, we're off!

There is nothing inherently wrong with this method. But it is worth our time to consider the consequences of students associating maximally controversial issues with always being put on the offensive. There are the fairly obvious ways that this association can stymie students' analysis. Any teacher who has managed debates this way recognizes that pivotal moment where all points have been shared, and all that's left for kids is to share them louder. And louder. And maybe now with profanity to punctuate their sincerity. It could be three minutes into the debate or 20. But we eventually reach the point where the only skills being practiced are speakers' loquaciousness and everyone else's endurance. Students aren't holding the issue up to new light or taking it apart. They are just arguing. This sparks other consequences for our classroom community; for instance, if Student A truly cares about an issue and Student B relentlessly attacks it—even while honoring all surface-level decorum—it will be hard for Student A to dispassionately just "move on" when the debate is over, especially if the topic is visceral to them, while only academic to their partner. Furthermore, when these debates get heated, students are encouraged to spend capital that they might not have built up. Subtle jokes to cut the tension are misunderstood. Worst intentions are assumed all around.

It doesn't have to be this way. First, we ought not to default to putting kids immediately on the offensive. To encourage a more deliberative framing, we need to *encourage students to ask these questions*:

- Before the debate: What *don't* I know about this issue? How might that impact this upcoming debate?

- During the debate: What points is my opponent making? Which are weakest? Which are strongest? What are the reasons behind those points, and what do I need to find out?

- After the debate: What have I learned from my opponent? (Even if I don't agree, what have I learned about their thinking?) What might a third-party observer say about our exchange?

Further, introducing a more deliberative debating framework is less likely to damage classroom relationships and, taken a step further, can help to strengthen them. For instance, we could *do these things*:

- Encourage students to "shout out" sound points made by their classmates during the debate.

- Link thoughtful debate prompts to a larger collaborative project so that students with different communication styles don't feel like the verbal debate was their only chance to weigh in. This not only lowers the stakes of any one classroom exchange, but it also gives students another opportunity to praise one another's contributions.

Most importantly, we should *remember two things*:

- **Debates need to be preceded with research, with preparation, and with practice on students' argumentation.** Remember, as *The Case for Contention* states, the parties to a dispute should be "fairly competent with respect to the question at issue" (Zimmerman & Robertson, 2017, p. 49). In other words, we need to fight the temptation to just sic the kids on each other ("You stand here. You stand here. Now go!") when they don't really know what they are talking about. Kids who are unprepared are more likely to embarrass themselves. They are more likely to weaponize stereotypes. They are more likely to personally attack classmates because they are ill-equipped to substantially engage opposing ideas. This can erode a classroom community, but proper preparation can help build it up.

- **Debate the silly stuff too.** Why would that character do that? Did the author really need that chapter? Was the movie version really as bad as the teacher says it is? Let the kids debate issues that they can joke about in the hallway after class. When the issues being debated are not maximally controversial— when the emotional investment is not as heavy—debates allow kids to be funny, to be mock-serious, to act things out. We discover the quirkiest traits in our students during silly debates. And more importantly, they discover the same quirks in each other, which only strengthens the classroom community.

It is also worth thinking about the different forms that debate can take. Some that we employ include the following:

- **Pop-Up Debate.** In this structure, Dave Stuart asks every student to participate one or two times and to simply "pop-up" at their desk to speak. Dave tries to hold a pop-up debate in his classes at least two times per month, as this allows classes to progress into deeper levels of skill. These are not graded conversations in Dave's classroom; rather, they are live demonstrations of a variety of literacy skills, including use of evidence, use of reasoning, paraphrasing, counterargument, and speech delivery.

- **Support a _____ Debate.** Matt Johnson will sometimes pull contrasting literary analysis and different takes on some controversial moments in literature. What is going on with the mock mule funeral in *Their Eyes Were Watching God*? Why does Fitzgerald keep randomly mentioning Owl Eyes or T. J. Eckleburg in *The Great Gatsby*? The class will then align themselves with one viewpoint or another and debate on its behalf. This is a great

A deeper dive into pop-up debates

way to model what good literary analysis looks like and can be more inviting for students who get nervous giving their own take in front of the class. Sometimes, Matt asks other ELA teachers in the school to give their anonymous thoughts on some scene or controversy. Students love to try to use context clues to figure out which teacher is connected to which take, and the big reveal of who said what elicits a great cheer.

What Role Does Celebration Play in Building Community in the Classroom?

Classroom celebrations, seemingly by definition, often happen at the end of things: at the end of a unit, a quarter, a semester, the year. But "we made it!" celebrations are only one type of celebration, and alone, they likely won't lead to a culture of celebration—a culture that can act as a potent fuel for the students' efforts during all sorts of hard work. At every step of learning, there is an opportunity to cheer and celebrate one's gains and choices, and we've found that the more we celebrate, the less room there is in our classrooms for malaise or toxic competitiveness to seep in.

AUTHENTIC WAYS TO BUILD IN CELEBRATION AND THANKS

- **Incorporate peer response regularly.** The peer response process gives regular chances for students to celebrate the draft versions of each other's unique ideas, incisive thesis statements, funny wordplay, and rich metaphors. Peer response will be covered more broadly in Chapter 3, but it should be noted for now that the approach of these regular peer response sessions is not what we experienced in our collegiate days where we did "writers workshops" that consisted of our peers tearing apart our drafts, pointing out everything that was cliché or stuffy or whatever. Instead, we seek to find ways for student response to fellow classmates' writing to have as much celebrating and learning from works as it has discussion of what needs work.

- **Make theater a part of your classroom.** In Matt Kay's class, not only do kids read plays that require acting, but they can also make micro-theater out of just about every text they read. If we make space for dramatic interpretation, kids could be "at a show" every week, with all the applause and imaginary tossed bouquets that come with it.

- **Make student sharing (and celebrating) of student work a regular feature of the class.** The quick-sharing protocols given earlier in the chapter (the cascading quick-share and anonymous share) allow for another quick way to celebrate the gains and work of students. Taking a minute to celebrate wonderful word choice, lines, moments, and ideas takes almost no time at all, and yet it can add a meaningful additional layer of celebration.

- **Make publishing a natural last step for writing projects**, which can include making a classroom poetry collection, entering student work into youth playwriting or essay competitions, submitting it to literary magazines, entering the *New York Times* student contests, or even encouraging students to self-publish through Amazon Marketplace (which Matt Kay's students have done—it's so cool to see kids' writing make them some spending money!). Not only is every magazine acceptance, contest win, or dollar earned a cause for celebration, but every poem, story, or play published also gives your students' proud grandmoms and grandads another reason to spoil them.

• **Use micro-conferences to celebrate student gains.** Conferences are often thought about in the context of working on a piece of student writing or checking in on a student's choice of reading books, but Matt Johnson seeks to have at least two or three micro-conferences (or brief conferences lasting no more than one or two minutes) each semester. In them, he checks in with students briefly on the edges of class time as they shuffle in or out—or even during independent reading or drafting time—to specifically celebrate a gain they made. Similar to Dave Stuart's Moments of Genuine Connection (see Chapter 2), Matt keeps track of these quick personal moments of celebration to ensure every student gets a few each semester.

• **Make a big deal over small wins.** It's not uncommon to see Dave Stuart model joyful learning by making a brief exclamation about something "small but good" that he sees a learner doing. In each of the following examples, Dave's goal is to send a quick signal to the class that learning and growing as a reader, writer, speaker, listener, and thinker is a joy-filled process:

  • "Miquel, look at how you used an em dash there! That is a perfect spot for one—just the right break in your sentence. Well done!"
  • "Hey everyone, did you hear what Ivy just did there? She paraphrased what Hunter said, and then she added to his argument with evidence of her own. Nice move, Ivy!"
  • "Dominic, that's what we call an 'insight' right there, my man! Wow. Did anyone else see that in the text?"

Notes

HOW DO I CULTIVATE MOTIVATION IN AN ELA CLASSROOM?

Just before the start of the pandemic, researchers at the Yale Center for Emotional Intelligence asked over 21,000 American high school students how they felt about school. The results were devastating: Over 75 percent of respondents indicated negative emotions regarding school, and the most frequently cited feelings were being bored, tired, and stressed (Khan, 2020).

This isn't just a high school problem either. According to a recent Gallup survey, student engagement drops consistently starting in the secondary grades. In Grade 5, it's at 74 percent; in Grade 8, it's 45 percent; by Grade 12, it's at 34 percent (Calderon & Yu, 2017). And this was all pre-Covid. Given what we've seen in our classes, the pandemic probably didn't do much to remedy these disturbing traits and likely made them worse.

The best ELA lesson in the world, when given to a room full of bored, tired, and stressed-out students, is not going to deliver as much learning as it ought to. And having a room full of students who feel like that is going to certainly drain the teacher who is trying to provide that excellent instruction.

This chapter endeavors to get to the root of this core question: **How do we cultivate motivating classroom contexts—places where our students *want* to do the work of learning and want to do it with *care*?** This is a question we pursue on behalf of our students and ourselves because even though disengagement and negative emotions are apparently widespread in secondary schools, this need not be the case in our classrooms. We can cultivate motivation in our ELA classrooms, but it takes some understanding of what true motivation is and how we can encourage it in our students—and it takes some work. Here's how we're breaking it down for you:

- [ ] **What is at the heart of student motivation?**
- [ ] **What are the best methods for developing credibility as a teacher?**
- [ ] **How do I help students to see the value of literacy?**
- [ ] **How do I help students believe that their effort will lead to success?**
- [ ] **What are the best methods for developing efficacy in a classroom?**
- [ ] **How can I help students develop a sense of belonging in our classroom?**
- [ ] **How do grades relate to student motivation?**
- [ ] **How can I build strong relationships with all students?**
- [ ] **What should I keep in mind about classroom management and student motivation?**
- [ ] **What is culturally responsive pedagogy, and how does it relate to student motivation?**
- [ ] **What common engagement methods don't work as well as they're touted?**

What Is at the Heart of Student Motivation?

At its core, our interest in student motivation can be boiled down to a two-part question: How do we help our students to (1) do the work of mastery-seeking and (2) do that work with care? In the middle and high school ELA classroom, the specific goal we seek is deepening each student's aptitude in reading, writing, speaking, listening, and thinking, while also broadening their understanding of the world and the people who live within it. For this to happen optimally, we need way more than compliant learning behaviors; we need learning behaviors driven by a fire in the fullness of themselves. We can't coerce this kind of work and care for our students; we can only cultivate the conditions, much like a thoughtful gardener prepares a flower bed in the spring, in the hope that, given the right ingredients, such motivation will sprout within their wills.

Specifically, we can seek this goal through the creation of courses, assignments, conversations, and spaces that cultivate five key beliefs: Credibility, Value, Belonging, Effort, and Efficacy.

Belief	What It Sounds Like in the Heart of a Student
Credibility	My teachers are good at their job. They know what they're doing. They care about me, as a learner and a person. They've got what it takes to help me succeed.
Value	This work matters to my life. This discussion is interesting. This reading is going to be useful someday. This essay is shaping me into a person more capable of flourishing long term.
Effort	If I focus on sentence variation, I'll become a better writer. If I attend to eliminating distracting behaviors while I speak, I'll become a better speaker. If I work smart and hard, I'll grow in my mastery of the fundamentals of literacy.
Efficacy	I can succeed at this unit. I can contribute to this conversation. I can become a better writer.
Belonging	People like me read. It makes sense that I'm engaging in a conversation in class right now. I fit here in this writing community. I'm a literate person on the path to deeper literacy.

From a strategic standpoint, it's useful to think of these as a mountain, as in Figure 2.1.

Figure 2.1 Key Beliefs

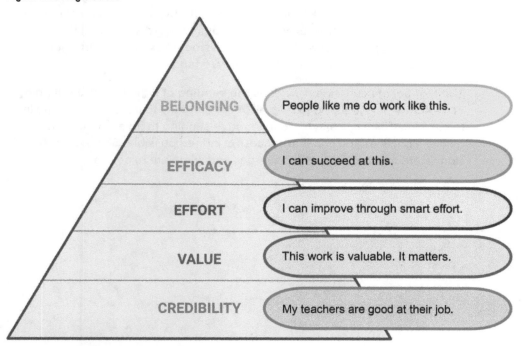

Start your student motivation journey from the bottom. First, get good at cultivating Credibility in your room; it's got a super-high effect size in John Hattie's research (Hattie, 2012), and it'll make your life a lot more pleasant. If you get overwhelmed by the five key beliefs, just focus on this one until you're feeling strong in it.

Then, get good at cultivating Value because if students don't value the reading or writing or speaking or thinking you'll ask them to do, why would they care about the role of Effort in getting better at that work or whether they'll succeed at it (Efficacy), or whether they identify with that kind of work (Belonging)?

We'll examine all of those in this chapter. But before we zoom in, here are critical things to know from the research on these beliefs:

- **These beliefs are malleable.** At the classroom level, teachers have a measurable effect on each of these beliefs in each of their students. In other words, none of our students' hearts are immovable; none of our students should be labeled in Sharpie as "unmotivated." This can help us to view problems with student motivation as solvable puzzles rather than permanent problems.

- **These beliefs are context dependent.** Our actions, interactions, lessons, curricula, activities, posters, and pedagogies can all positively or negatively influence these five key beliefs and thereby help or hinder student motivation.

- **These beliefs are subintellectual.** It's not enough to get students to know about and articulate these beliefs; for example, over the past several decades the concept of growth mindset (which we're calling the Effort belief) has become ubiquitous in schools, and yet there is "an absence of data showing that heightened awareness of mind-set principles has contributed to an increase in a growth mind-set among students over the past 20 years" (Fotuhi, 2020). Findings like this suggest that it's better to skip teaching students about these beliefs and head straight toward cultivating them quietly as you go about your work as a classroom ELA teacher. In a sense, the five key beliefs are caught more than they're taught.

- **Think of beliefs cultivation work as the sending of signals, not the flipping of switches.** You're trying to help all of our students to believe in their ability to succeed (Efficacy), and to do this, you're sending them as many high-quality signals as you can that success is indeed possible. Some of these signals are verbal, some are nonverbal, and some are experiential.

Notes

What Are the Best Methods for Developing Credibility as a Teacher?

Credibility	My teachers are good at their job. They know what they're doing. They care about me, as a learner and a person. They've got what it takes to help me succeed.

There's been a ton written on teacher credibility in the past decade, and for good reason: In John Hattie's (2012) *Visible Learning* meta-analysis, credibility has over twice the effect size of an average intervention. And it's also popular because it passes the smell test: Do we really learn more from those we believe in? Our own experiences both as students and teachers point to a resounding *yes*.

There are several models for understanding what goes into students' belief in the credibility of their teacher, but we think the simplest to remember and act upon is CCP: care, competence, and passion, as detailed in Figure 2.2.

Figure 2.2 CCP: Care, Competence, and Passion

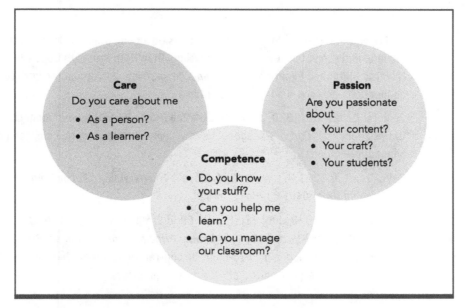

Source: Stuart (2018)

TO INFLUENCE THE CARE COMPONENT OF CREDIBILITY

When showing your students you care about them, you can do these things:

- **Track moments of genuine connection.** Get a clipboard, print a list of all your student rosters, and make it your goal to attempt a moment of genuine connection (MGC) with each student on the list. What we specifically mean by an MGC is a brief conversation (30–90 seconds long) where the teacher actively attempts to make the student feel valued, known, or respected.

What Are the Best Methods for Developing Credibility as a Teacher?

35

You won't always succeed in getting students to feel this way, but even the attempt can show them that you care.

- **Use "2×10" for the student in class you're having the hardest time connecting with.** First studied by Raymond Wlodkowski in the 1980s, 2×10 is simple: For two minutes straight on 10 consecutive days of class, have a nonacademic conversation with the student you're having the hardest time connecting with. Just like MGCs, these 2×10 conversations are best held right before or right after class or during a segment of independent practice in your lessons. In Wlodkowski's (1983) observations of classrooms using this intervention, 85 percent saw an improvement in overall class behavior. And you know what else likely happened? Students perceived that their teacher cared.

- **Say *hi* as the students enter the class**. A 2018 study of 10 middle school classrooms found that simply offering a positive greeting to students as they entered the door led to a 20 percent increase in engagement and a 9 percent decrease in behavior issues (Cook et al., 2018). The likely reason for the pretty remarkable return on an investment of a few scattered smiles and hellos? Our guess is that it reminded the students that the teacher did indeed care about them.

Great Resources

- Lori Desautels. (2018, July 18). Connections Go a Long Way for Students With Trauma: Initiating Short Personal Interactions May Help Students Cope With Adverse Childhood Experiences. *Edutopia*. https://www.edutopia.org/article/connections-go-long-way-students-trauma.

- Jennifer Gonzalez. (2020, July 16). Creating Moments of Genuine Connection Online [Podcast]. *Cult of Pedagogy*. https://www.cultofpedagogy.com/genuine-connection-online/.

- Dave Stuart Jr. (2018). Chapter 2 of *These 6 Things: How to Focus Your Teaching on What Matters Most*. Corwin.

- Dave Stuart Jr. (2020, July 21). *How to Build Strong Relationships With Students if You're Starting the Year Online: Principles and Practices* [Blog post]. https://davestuartjr.com/how-to-build-strong-relationships-with-students-if-youre-starting-the-year-online-principles-and-practices/.

TO INFLUENCE THE COMPETENCE COMPONENT OF CREDIBILITY

There's no instant way to grow competence in a job as hard as teaching, but there are some faster paths to efficiencies that far too few of us tread, including the following:

- Instead of allowing yourself to try to learn *everything* about teaching *all the time*, **decide on one particular area each month that you'd like to improve.** In the very book you're holding, each chapter could be one of these monthly areas! By focusing your improvement efforts in one area at a time, you'll destress yourself and quickly form pockets of expertise that will appear to the outside observer as impressive competence.

- Instead of relying on your own perception of how any particular strategy is working, **invite trusted colleagues into your class to give you another set of eyes.** They don't have to visit for more than a few minutes—just long enough to see your instruction from a different angle. Then, meet up over a coffee and chat about it, and don't forget to return the favor.

- **Be a passionate reader and a writer.** One of the great ironies of being an ELA teacher is that the reading and writing from class can crowd out personal reading and writing. When it comes to credibility, finding ways to maintain a vibrant reading and writing life outside of your school work is essential. Students can often sense if you are a true believer in reading and writing, and if they figure out that *you* aren't even bothering to read and write, it begs the question why should *they*? However, if they see you as a robust reader both in and out of class, it adds one more layer to your credibility. If you are worried about how to find the time to do that, check out Chapter 5.

TO INFLUENCE THE PASSION COMPONENT OF CREDIBILITY

- **When you're struggling with a unit that you're not passionate about, view it as a passion puzzle instead of a passion problem.** What angle can I take on this unit that allows me to authentically appreciate the learning process with my students? Sometimes, the angle might be the content; other times, it might be the students you're teaching; and still other times, it might be the craft of connecting the content to the students. Dave Stuart has a story he likes to tell about how he doesn't love Ray Bradbury's *Fahrenheit 451*. (Don't judge him too harshly. It's just a style thing for Dave.) He likes to tell the story because early in his career he realized that he could be open with his students about the stylistic complaints he had with the book—and it actually made many of the students appreciate the book more! Dave now loves this unit; he found an angle to passion through the things that were bothering him.

- **Find ways to bring passions into the classroom**. Jessyca Mathews of Carman-Ainsworth High School in Flint, Michigan, noticed that during her city's famous water crisis, her students, like her, felt a strong desire to say and do something to respond to everything being (and not being) said and done around them. Mathews eventually connected her class with Chicago-based artist Jan Tichy and the Eli and Edythe Broad Art Museum, leading to an interactive art installation of water pipes and youth poetry about the Flint Water Crisis (Stateside Staff, 2017). This experience led Mathews to found an activism in inquiry class, a senior-level elective where Mathews's students seek answers to problems they are passionate about through a deep study of the history and tactics of activists who came before them. They then use what they find to engage in their own activism, and the result is an experience that feeds both her students' passions and Mathews's own passion for empowering youth voices.

How Do I Help Students to See the Value of Literacy?

Value	This work matters to my life. This discussion is interesting. This reading is going to be useful someday. This essay is shaping me into a person more capable of flourishing long term.

If we've got Credibility working in our classroom, our next aim is to cultivate a deep sense of Value for the work of reading, writing, speaking, listening, and thinking that happens in a language arts classroom. What we want is for students to engage in the work of literacy willingly, not just because we've asked them to do it (Credibility) but because they personally value it.

We want our students to say things like, "I love reading!" or "Writing is useful," or "In-class debates are interesting." All of these are expressions of a fundamental belief in the Value of the work at hand.

An interesting thing about Value is that we arrive at it in individualized, unique ways. But there are a few broad categories that can help us think about cultivating robust value beliefs in our classroom: prosocial purpose, utility, relevance, and aesthetic enjoyment. A few things to note before we dive in:

- We want our aim to be a classroom that's flooded with value-rich signals. As a result, we want to pull from each of the broad categories as evenly as we can, so as not to overwork any one method for arriving at Value. In the late 1800s, British education philosopher Charlotte Mason gives a wise warning against playing toward single sources of value: "[The teacher] should know how to incite the child to effort through his desire of [praise], of excelling, of advancing, his desire of knowledge, his love of parents, his sense of duty, in such a way that no one set of motives be called unduly into play to the injury of the child's character" (Mason, 2017, p. 141). It's an interesting idea worth mulling over as we think about the diversity of approaches to Value that we use in our rooms.

- Although we've broken the following ideas down into categories, think of them as blended paints on a palette. In other words, prosocial purpose can also be relevant to a student; work that is meaningful can also be highly enjoyable.

- The highest goal we can have is for our students to conceive of learning as a valuable thing for all kinds of reasons. That's not just us saying that: Researchers Purdie and Hattie (2002) found that the more conceptions of learning that a student had, the more likely it was that the student did well in school.

PROSOCIAL PURPOSE

Prosocial purpose is "psychologese" for doing something because of how it may help someone else. In adolescents especially, prosocial purpose can be a powerful lever for cultivating Value in a given lesson or unit. Here are some ways to leverage prosocial purpose in our classrooms:

- **Make projects or essays public.** For a given writing assignment or unit, consider whether there might be a method for making the publication of the work something that expands beyond your classroom. Could an essay become a letter sent to someone who can make a difference in a particular field? Could a research paper become a call to action emailed to a local representative? In Dave Stuart's classroom, for a number of years students would complete an end-of-year passion project based on a student-driven fundraising drive for Charity: Water, a nonprofit that provides clean drinking water to people in developing nations. Each student identified their own means for communicating the water crisis and raising funds for a well.

- **Give real-life examples of folks who use literacy skills and knowledge to make the world a better place.** Bill Damon was a Stanford researcher who spent his career studying the development of purpose in young people. In his extensive studies, Damon found that one of the best avenues to cultivating purpose in a young person is giving them plenty of what he called "purpose exemplars"—adults driven by a sense of prosocial purpose (Damon, 2009).

RELEVANCE

Relevance is the effort to make a clear connection between a lesson, subject, or text to a student's interests or experiences outside of the classroom. In today's professional discourse around student motivation, relevance gets an outsized share of the attention. Before getting into some methods for cultivating Value via relevance, let's consider a drawback to this approach.

Importantly, we must keep in mind that it's easy to get into sticky circumstances when you start making assumptions about what will or won't be relevant to a student. For example, if the top song on the Billboard charts is a Taylor Swift serenade, that doesn't mean every student in the room is going to be Swiftie (or even know what that means). Secondary students in particular are often highly attuned to and easily offended by the moments where adults make assumptions about what is or isn't relevant to them.

So instead of assuming that all your students are listening to this artist or playing that video game, try these for cultivating Value via relevance:

- **The "Build Connections" intervention** published by Character Lab offers a simple protocol for helping students to generate their own relevance connections between the things they are learning in class and the things they value outside of it (view the QR in the margin to access this protocol). It essentially comes down to this:

  - Students brainstorm a list of things they value—goals, interests, hobbies—and then next to that list, they brainstorm a separate list of

Character Lab's "Build Connections" protocol

things they've learned in class recently, such as concepts, terms, projects, papers, assignments, and readings.

- Then, students look for any links they can think of between the two lists, drawing lines between the two. Here, it helps if they then explain a link or two to a partner and if the teacher asks for volunteers to share. The goal now is to jog as many connections as possible.
- Finally, students write about one of their connections. These two templates help:
  - _____ is connected to _____ because _____.
  - _____ could be important to my life because _____.

- **Incorporate open space into a lesson or unit.** In interviewing young writers for his book _Writing Unbound_ (2021), legendary teacher Tom Newkirk found that "a central theme in almost all the interviews was a craving for more open space" (p. 44). This makes sense in that we all understand at some level that our hours and cognition are limited, and thus we are drawn with unusual passion to those things we value. When we create open space for students to bring in what they value, we are in a sense inviting what they already value to our wider conversation, which in turn makes everything else in the conversation more interesting. Read on for more places we can add open space in our classes:

  - Invite students to share, analyze, and mimic texts _they_ love, not just texts _you_ love. If you are examining descriptive word choice, that can often be done as well in that beat-up, favorite book they've read 20 times as it can in a text you love.
  - Allow students to have more say in the construction of their papers and projects. Not every paper and project needs to stem from a narrow prompt (more on this in Chapter 4). Teaching students how to pursue their own interests and passions is a valuable skill.
  - Give students the option to choose their own levels for some topics. For example, in Matt Johnson's classes, students often come in with a wide range of understanding concerning how to use commas, so Matt gives them two potential options when it comes to learning about them: the basics or the stylistics of using commas. (Our online companion, resources.corwin.com/answersELA, contains two downloadable examples to show how Matt J. teaches commas.)
  - Allow students to submit requests for future current events mini-lessons or articles of the week (Gallagher, 2009).

UTILITY

Utility is a fancy way of saying "usefulness." It's what students are asking with this classic question: "Hey, when are we ever going to use iambic pentameter in real life?" "When are we ever going to use this" may make us bristle because we know what we are doing is valuable, but what they are really saying is, "Hey, I'm having a hard time valuing this work we're doing. Can you help?" And that is a question worth answering thoughtfully. As with relevance, it is worth noting that utility shouldn't be the only way to cultivate Value, but when it's not too much of a reach, utility is a good angle to pursue in your efforts to cultivate this belief in your classroom.

To make utility clear to students, try these methods:

- **Select excerpts from** *Writing: A Ticket to Work or a Ticket Out* (National Commission on Writing, 2004); **read and discuss them with your students.** In this fascinating and freely available survey of employers across the sectors, writing skill was consistently cited as an important factor in hiring and promotion decisions. Dave Stuart has had good discussions based on this activity with students who plan on pursuing work in fields such as manufacturing, construction, or the like. Often, these students, upon reading and considering excerpts from the report's executive summary, will say things like, "Well sure, my dad is shift leader at his job, and he's got to write a report every day after work."

- **Turn the question "When will we use this in real life?" back on students to answer.** In his classes, before students are assigned the first choice reading section, big paper, or poem, Matt Johnson asks students why they think we read books of our choosing, write essays, and engage in poetry, and the class then makes a big list. Matt is always amazed at how readily students will list incredibly thoughtful reasons for even more abstract topics like poetry, and since he started doing this, he hasn't heard "How will this help me in the real world?" in years!

- **Remind students how useful writing and public speaking will be to their non-work lives.** Matt Kay often reminds students that a command of descriptive and figurative language will help them write their sweethearts the best little love notes or eventual wedding vows. (He gets a few reliable laughs every year retelling the story of his college side hustle writing Valentine messages to impress his classmates' significant others.) He takes a similar tack with public speaking, especially during rhetoric units. Students are reminded that they are often trying to convince folks to do something (their parents!) or that others are trying to convince *them* to do something (again, their parents!). They are excited to learn both the rhetorical techniques and how to counter them.

 Equity and Access

Researchers Chris Hulleman and Judith Harackiewicz (2009) found, in a study of ninth-grade science students, that when students wrote monthly on how the topics from class applied to their lives, those with low expectations coming into the year scored .80 grade points higher than a control group of similar students who wrote about the topics from class generally. This study was striking in that this short meditation upon the utility of class barely made a ripple for students who had high expectations, but for those who didn't think they could do it—likely because they'd struggled in science in years prior— the effect size was nearly off the charts!

ENJOYMENT

An often overlooked path to Value is enjoyment. Sometimes, teachers lose sight of the fact that there is deep joy to be had in growing as a reader, writer, speaker, and person—and that is exactly what you and I have to offer.

To boost enjoyment, try these ideas:

- **Say a million times per school year that learning is good because learning is good.** The idea here is that students are accustomed to hearing teachers say things like, "Well, you'll need this in the real world" (utility) or "Well, this assignment is kind of like TikTok" (relevance)—actually, they don't say that last one, but you get the gist. But it's rarer for a student to hear a person who is gently and joyfully repetitive about the idea that growing in literacy is one of life's greatest joys.

- **Model enjoyment.** Every once and while, get lost in loving a particular sentence or character or idea. There is a line where doing this too often turns the spotlight on the teacher in a way that is not particularly useful, but to show your genuine enjoyment of something from time to time helps to model enjoyment and add to credibility.

- **(Cautiously) use humor that fits you and your class culture.** Everyone likes to laugh, and middle and high school students are no exception. The thing is, humor is individualized, and one person's cause for hilarity could be another's humiliation. For the sake of Credibility and Belonging in our classrooms, then, we want to be really thoughtful about the humor that we use with secondary students. Sarcasm in particular can be a risky form of humor with students; while teachers often chuckle when a joke they make goes over the head of a group of students, placing ourselves in our students' shoes makes this a bit less funny. Humor that's light and playful is often the safest path to making class a bit more enjoyable without the risk of offending someone unintentionally.

Notes

How Do I Help Students Believe That Their Effort Will Lead to Success?

Effort	If I focus on sentence variation, I'll become a better writer. If I attend to eliminating distracting behaviors while I speak, I'll become a better speaker. If I work smart and hard, I'll grow in my mastery of the fundamentals of literacy.

The Effort belief is more commonly called growth mindset. We don't call it that, though, because growth mindset is one of those terms in education that's been "buzzwordified"—that is, linguistically extended to mean so many things to so many people that mentioning it in a conversation is almost sure to result in folks walking away with different ideas of what was just discussed.

But just because the term has been extended doesn't mean that the core idea isn't powerful: At the end of the day, people are unlikely to try something that they think is bound to lead to their stagnation or failure. This is central to the Effort belief.

To help students believe their effort will pay off, try these:

- **Teach the most effective kinds of effort.** Don't forget the fundamentals. The late, legendary UCLA basketball coach John Wooden famously taught his nationally recruited college basketball athletes to put on their socks and tie their shoes effectively on the first day of practice. This example sounds absurd, but it's illustrative when you research Wooden's methods further. Basically, Wooden viewed his role not as that of a coach so much as that of a teacher. He relentlessly taught and structured practice for his players around the fundamental skills upon which game-time success is constructed. As a result, Wooden's teams were famously sound on the fundamentals, and this is one of many factors that led his teams toward a yet-unmatched string of national college basketball titles. We want to teach students "how to tie their shoes"—not condescendingly, but instead lovingly, passionately. How do I find a good spot to read where I live? How do I take notes in preparation for an essay? How do I think better about writing the start of an essay or story? Any effort that we expect of students is effort we ought to teach and model—but remember: Don't let a hyperfocus on fundamentals get in the way of doing the actual cool stuff like writing authentic poetry or creative stories. Even Coach Wooden let players scrimmage during practice.

- **Do compare and contrast.** Learning is often like the advance or retreat of a glacier: While on rare occasions there can be dramatic moments of transformation where in a moment the old you comes crashing down to reveal a sparkling new version underneath, 99 percent of the time change happens so slowly as to be unobservable. Still, even when there have been no dramatic moments in a week or month, those slow, incremental changes that make up most of a student's learning do add up over time. Many students may not see this, so it is worth drawing their attention to it from time to time through comparing and contrasting earlier work with later work. This can

How Do I Help Students Believe That Their Effort Will Lead to Success?

43

take the form of a teacher comment that compares a new thesis to one from the semester before or notes how the reading levels of independent reading books have grown with each new selection. It can also take the form of asking students to compare and contrast themselves by having them revise and reflect upon earlier work through midsemester or midyear reflections (more on these in Chapter 4) or through the creation of portfolios.

- **When students fail despite working hard, intervene strategically.** In these situations, you can make a lot of motivational progress by getting specific information from students about what kinds of work they did and specific instruction on what kinds of work might work better next time. For example, it's common before tests for students to "read over their notes," but such activities prove ineffective at preparing students for assessments. Instead, students are better off quizzing themselves on learned material, as the act of requiring one's mind to pull up learned information demonstrably improves the mind's ability to pull it up subsequently.

- **Notice when students succeed gradewise despite not working particularly hard.** In these situations, we should be careful to not to try shaming our way into students' attention with stuff like, "I expected better effort from you!" Yet it's important to recognize some missed opportunities that result in students' work not meeting its potential. This feedback need not be grade-centric. For instance, we might challenge certain students to excel on a particular creative writing skill—"I want to see some dynamite dialogue from you! You tease the ability to do it in this other part," or "Next time, bring this story home! You really got me hooked with this exposition, and the rising action deserves a chef's kiss! But then it fizzled a bit, right? Bring it home with the same heat!"

Notes

What Are the Best Methods for Developing Efficacy in a Classroom?

Efficacy	I can succeed at this unit. I can contribute to this conversation. I can become a better writer.

Efficacy is, in short, the belief that you can succeed, and when thinking about it, there is one huge thing you have to keep in mind: You can only get so far trying to talk students into it. If you try to tell students 100 times that they can read and understand a book, they'll likely only persist through failure a time or two before deciding that this kind of thing just isn't going to happen for them.

What you've got to do instead is *teach* the students how to read and understand the book! This is how Efficacy is best cultivated: through real-deal, in-the-classroom success.

If students have or begin to have a history of writing successfully in school, they are students who will tend to believe in their ability to succeed at the writing assignment you've just introduced. So when it comes to efficacy, our job is in large part to help students build a string of successful academic experiences. Here are some ways to do that:

- **Clearly define success with students at varying scales of time.** What does it mean to be successful this school year? This unit? This lesson? In many schools, it's become commonplace for teachers to post "success criteria" prominently for each lesson and to mention them at the start of the lesson. Done right, such success criteria are boons to the Efficacy belief because they make success clear.

- **At the start of a unit, lead students in a WOOP exercise.** Ask students to come up with a *wish* for the unit ahead. Then, have them picture what the best possible *outcome* would be for them if they were to achieve that goal. Next, have them picture what the biggest *obstacle*—within their control— is. And finally, have students write an if/then *plan* for making progress toward their goal, even when the obstacle comes up. In numerous studies, researcher Gabrielle Oettingen has demonstrated that this brief "mental contrasting with implementation intentions" exercise significantly increases the frequency of goal-striving behaviors (Duckworth et al., 2013). Dave has provided an example from his personal workbook in Figure 2.3.

- **Find and highlight meaningful moments of student competence.** In his book *Embarrassment: And the Emotional Underlife of Learning,* Tom Newkirk (2017) discusses how a great many students come into our classes already certain that they will not be successful. Newkirk's answer for working with students who have already thrown in the Efficacy towel before class even starts is that the only way to counter those narratives, given the long and troubled histories that often lie behind them, is to introduce new and plausible counternarratives *that are very clearly based in reality*. He asserts that "self-esteem cannot be built upon the wind or empty assurances—it requires

Figure 2.3 Example WOOP page from Dave's notebook

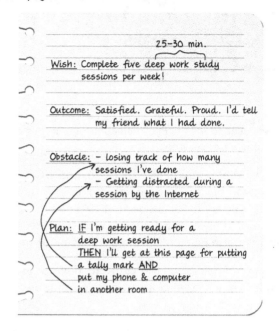

25–30 min.

Wish: Complete five deep work study
sessions per week!

Outcome: Satisfied. Grateful. Proud. I'd tell
my friend what I had done.

Obstacle: – losing track of how many
sessions I've done
– Getting distracted during a
session by the Internet

Plan: IF I'm getting ready for a
deep work session
THEN I'll get at this page for putting
a tally mark AND
put my phone & computer
in another room

objective and publicly acknowledged demonstrations of competence, being good at something" (2017, p. 45). In other words, if we want students to believe they can do it, vague and generalized half-truths won't be enough. We need to ask *What is this student doing well?* just as clearly and loudly as we ask *What help does she need?* And when we find the things that students are legitimately good at, we need to bring them to their attention just as loudly as we bring up criticism, and we need to do it again and again. If we can do this effectively, eventually these moments can form tangible kernels from which new and more positive reading, writing, and thinking identities might grow.

- **At the start of a school year, ask students to picture what kind of person they'd like to be someday.** Periodically link this big picture image with the work you're doing in the classroom. (Dave Stuart likes to have students record these big-picture goals on First Day Index Cards—see Chapter 1.)

- **When planning your units, break summative assessments (e.g., essays, projects, tests) into their smallest chunks and help students one chunk at a time.** This degree of scaffolding is challenging, given the different ability and knowledge levels present in every middle and secondary ELA classroom. However, few things are as predictive of summative assessment motivation as preceding student growth via formative work.

Great Resources

- Character Lab. (2022). WOOP for Classrooms. https://characterlab. org/activities/woop-for-classrooms/.

- Dave Stuart Jr. (2015, January 21). A Simple, Powerful Tweak on the First Day of School Index Card Activity. https://davestuartjr.com/ index-card-first-day-activity/.

How Can I Help Students Develop a Sense of Belonging in Our Classroom?

Belonging	People like me read. It makes sense that I'm engaging in a conversation in class right now. I fit here in this writing community. I'm a literate person on the path to deeper literacy.

Belonging comes down to whether I sense that who I am fits with where I'm at. That "where I'm at" piece is complex; it includes not just the peers I'm with or the physical space I'm in but also the topic we're learning about, the type of assignment we're working on, the level of success I had doing similar work last week, and so on.

In adolescents, the mind is especially concerned with identity–context fit. When this sense of fit isn't present—in other words, when a sense of belonging isn't there for a student—it's like that student has a background application running in their mind that's hogging up lots of energy and power. So we want to cultivate the Belonging belief not just because it's the right thing to do—because *all* students deserve to learn in places where they sense that they belong—but also because it is strategically necessary. No student will optimally learn when a part of their mental energy is being drained by questions of whether or not they fit, whether or not other folks think they fit, and so on.

Here's the baseline strategy: Because the classroom context is fluid, we want to send as many signals as possible to every single one of our students that they, specifically, belong here.

This is part of what's at the heart of culturally responsive teaching. But it's also at the heart of the following common strategies used by middle and high school ELA teachers to cultivate Belonging in classrooms:

- **Early and often, seek to help students build reading and writing identities.** Find the easiest path for students to begin doing the reading and writing that readers and writers do. New Hampshire teacher–author Penny Kittle is one of many masters at this. She routinely guides reluctant readers into an initial independent reading book that's highly engaging and highly accessible, and then she slowly coaches students into selecting more challenging or complex texts. Penny shared an example at a conference in Denver: She sensed that a student needed to gain confidence and interest in reading. First, the student read Kwame Alexander's books *The Crossover, Rebound*, and *Swing* and followed that with a book club about *The Poet X* by Elizabeth Acevedo; all of these are written in verse, an accessible format, but tell stories that are age-appropriate and engaging for a teenage reader. The student then asked for Penny's recommendation, and Penny said *Between the World and Me*, by Ta-Nehisi-Coates, which Penny selected because the book "is a letter—which is a friendly form. [The student] then read *Sing, Unburied, Sing*, which was the hardest lift—multiple narrators, movements forward and backward in time, complexity in relationships between narrators—but [the student] hung in there, tracking plot in her notebook to increase her own understanding" (P. Kittle, personal communication, September 8, 2021). By finding a path for the student to do the work of reading in a way that she valued, Penny enabled the student to make a massive jump in reading ability—going from *The Crossover* to *Sing, Unburied, Sing*—and develop a genuine, evidence-based reader's identity along the way.

- **Make sure that you are keeping track of whether you've attempted to connect with each student on your roster.** Middle and high school class rosters are larger than elementary ones, which means most of us end up with anywhere from 100 to 200 students in our care each semester. If we leave our attempts at moments of genuine connection (MGCs; see p. 51) up to chance, we end up missing students—our biases and habits and limited awareness make this inevitable. But a simple tool, such as a clipboard with every one of your students' names on a single page and checkmarks for each MGC, can help keep us signaling to *all* students that they are valued, known, and respected.

- **Work inside yourself to ensure that you genuinely do value, know, and respect each one of your students.** We've never met a teacher who perfectly got along with every student on the roster; people are different, and this can lead to tension or annoyance. Also when students present instructional or behavioral challenges, our sense of efficacy can be quietly threatened, and this can lead us to consciously or unconsciously avoid thinking about or interacting with certain students as much as we need to. Because of these realities, we recommend doing a periodic self-check:

  - Are any of my students annoying me right now? What's at the root of that? What could I do to make it better? What else is there to this student that makes me glad that they are in my classroom?
  - Are any of my students really struggling right now? How do I feel about my ability to meet them in that struggle? Am I trying to be superhuman or a savior with them? Am I neglecting to try new things to serve them?
  - Questions like this have nuanced and complex answers, but in our practices, we find that reflecting along these lines helps to keep our hearts fresh *for* each of our students.

- **Work to reduce stereotype threat.** In 1995, researchers Steele and Aronson showed in several experiments that Black college freshmen and sophomores did not perform as well as white students on standardized tests *when their race was emphasized*. But when race was not emphasized on the test, the researchers found that Black students performed better or equivalently with white students. From this, Steele and Aronson inferred that performance in academic settings can be harmed when students are made aware that their behavior might be interpreted through the lens of negative racial stereotypes. Since then, researchers have found similar effects for minoritized groups in other settings (e.g., with young girls whose gender has been emphasized prior to a math task [Ambady et al., 2001], or whites when compared with Asian men in mathematics [Aronson et al., 1999]). To mitigate these effects, researchers encourage individuals to think of themselves as multifaceted and complex and for those around them to emphasize high standards with assurances about the capability to meet them. As teachers, we can help in both regards. We can bake high expectations, unwavering support, and reminders and celebrations of student complexity in everything we do, from the assignments we create to the feedback we provide.

How Do Grades Relate to Student Motivation?

The five key beliefs lie at the heart of student motivation, but other factors weigh heavily upon it as well. The most common of these factors is grades—arguably the most recognizable motivator we have in our schools. But here's a critical understanding about grades in the secondary literacy classroom: If all that's getting a child to do the work of learning is grades, then the child is poorly motivated. What we want is for our students to be invested with their hearts into the work of improving as readers, writers, thinkers, speakers, and people. We don't want them incentivized or coerced into doing this because we believe that becoming a literate person is one of life's best journeys and greatest rewards.

So how can we approach grades so that they support what we are trying to do with our students?

Grades will be discussed more in Chapter 3, but broadly speaking, there are three main camps around grading these days:

- Traditional grading

- Standards-based grading

- Ungrading (or no grading)

Now, folks who deep dive into the grading literature will (rightly) take issue with those three categories. They are oversimplifications, in this case intentionally so. Our point in laying them out so simply is that, while your method for grading is important, your grasp of the five key beliefs is *more* important. So often, teachers get stuck on small details with their grading systems, losing sight of bigger things like a student's sense of belonging or value. While we each have our own personal approach to grading and ungrading (more on specific systems in Chapter 3), we have seen classrooms with all three models that are filled with belonging, self-efficacy, student belief in the value of the work and that they can succeed with effort, and teaching that is widely viewed by the students as credible. We have also seen classrooms with all three models that were missing many of these things.

That is why we encourage you to spend *some* time figuring out the right grading model for you but then to return to the five key beliefs. With that said, here are some things to keep in mind regarding grading and its impact on student motivation:

  What we want is for our students to be invested with their hearts into the work of improving as readers, writers, thinkers, speakers, and people.

MOTIVATION

- **If a student or parent gives you the impression that all they care about is the grade, be wary of denigrating the student in your heart.** While it can be frustrating to work with learners who seem solely motivated by the grade, we must keep in mind that folks don't simply choose to be grades-driven; they are situated within a system that heavily suggests that this is the way to approach school. View these kinds of situations as opportunities to practice your craft as a literacy evangelist—becoming a competent reader, writer, speaker, listener, and thinker is a gateway to all manner of good things, now and in the future.

- **Frequently remind grade-oriented students that mastery is the most reliable path to better grades.** Dave tells students that if their focus is on mastery, over the long term their grades will follow, and he communicates this to parents as well. This path does come with an obvious caveat: You have to create the conditions in your classroom for mastery to truly lead to an improved grade. Wherever you see obstacles to this—for example, policies against essay revision—make changes where you can and advocate for changes where you lack the authority to do it unilaterally. This will help students and families internalize the idea that the learning is the point.

- **Consider teaching your students about lead and lag indicators.** This is a concept from *The 4 Disciplines of Execution* (McChesney et al., 2012). The most common goals in life—get a good job, build a good family, make the world a better place, and so on—are *lag* indicators. Once you see whether you've arrived at these goals, it's too late to do anything about the situation. *Lead* indicators, in contrast, are those actions and measurements you can take today that make it more likely that you will reach those lag indicators later. And the good thing with lead indicators is that you (or your students) can act on them right now! No need to wait to see how things work out. In a middle or high school ELA classroom, this might look like this:

Lag	Lead
I want to be a stronger reader.	• I add at least two unfamiliar words from my reading into my vocabulary tracker each day. • I read recreationally for at least 20 minutes each night. • I make note of the questions I have when I'm reading a challenging text, and I use resources (peers, teacher, the internet) to seek answers to these questions.
I want to be a stronger writer.	• I keep a log of the feedback my teacher gives me on my writing. • I write a page in my journal each night, labeled "Observations From the Day."
I want to be a stronger speaker.	• I strike up one conversation with someone I don't know well each day, trying to keep the conversation going for two minutes. • I participate in class, even when it's not required. • I ask at least one question in at least one class each day.

Here's the key takeaway we want you to get from this section: When students or families seem primarily motivated by grades, it's a five-key-beliefs issue that we should be unsurprised by but concerned about. We don't want to belittle anyone who is in this motivational situation, but at the same time, for the sake of maximizing learning and enjoyment in the literacy classroom, we do want to steadily attempt to create a culture where learning and growth—not grades—are the point.

For more on grading, check out p. 81.

How Can I Build Strong Relationships With All Students?

There are at least four ways in which strong teacher–student relationships positively impact student motivation:

1. Credibility: Specifically, when teachers have strong relationships with their students, they make it apparent that they care about them as people and learners.

2. Belonging: When a learning space is made relationally safe by strong teacher–student relationships, students are more likely to sense that their identities fit within that academic context.

3. Trauma alleviation: One of the most powerful factors in alleviating trauma is a relationship with a caring adult (Merrill, 2020).

4. Teacher motivation: While relationships aren't the point of schooling, they are one of its greatest rewards. When teachers feel relationally rewarded for their work, the strength required for the job is much easier to access.

It's clear we want strong teacher–student relationships in the middle and high school ELA classroom. How do we develop them?

First, *don't* do the superhero teacher thing that we all did when starting out: Classroom doors wide open during every lunch period and prep block and every day after school for a few hours. We know from experience that doing this will lead to a lot of great relationships with the students, but from a sustainability standpoint, this is insanely time intensive. While it feels great to build these time-intensive relationships with students, allocating your personal time toward hanging out with students means missing opportunities to respond to student work, ask experienced colleagues specific questions about how to improve one's craft, go out and find the right mentor texts, read research, or maybe—most importantly—take time to decompress and reflect.

Instead, we encourage leaning into proven teacher–student relationship builders that aren't so time intensive. Dave Stuart no longer spends every free moment hanging with students, and yet he has strong working relationships with nearly all of his students each school year—and pleasant ones with all the rest—thanks to a simple, unoriginal intervention called **Tracking Moments of Genuine Connection (MGCs)**.

- *Tracking*—You've got to have a method for keeping track, lest you allow your biases and blind spots to keep you from working the intervention with every student.

- *Moments*—Instead of leaving relationship-building as an open-ended feature of your room, you're seeking 30- to 60-second interactions with students in which you attempt to make them feel valued, known, and respected.

of Genuine—It's difficult to make a student feel valued, known, and respected if you don't actually value, know, and respect them. This is where the inner work of teaching is required—when you sense an internal block with a student, you've got to mine into that and try to figure out what's going on.

Connection—As finite creatures, we can't guarantee that a given interaction will make a person feel valued, known, and respected. All we can do is attempt it. That's why we keep these brief—so that we're getting more attempts per year.

It usually makes sense to attempt these at any of these times:

- Right before class

- At the very start of class (e.g., see Matt Kay's Burn 5 strategy, Chapter 1)

- During writer or reader conference sessions

- Right after class

Moments of genuine connection aren't the only efficient way to build these relationships either. Some other simple yet effective ways include these:

- Learn every name and how to pronounce it, and then greet each student by name when they come into class.

- Conduct short periodic interest surveys so you know what makes kids tick. These can be informal ("I'm curious what you think about . . .") or more assessment-like ("To practice parallel structure, do a short freewrite on something you are passionate about").

- Make positive feedback and encouragement part of your language, noting a specific thing a student has offered the class or has accomplished personally.

- Reconnect with a student who has been absent. Remind them that you're happy to see them back in class. Ask how you can support them in catching up.

- Hold reserved space for 2×10 conversations (Wlodkowski, 1983) with a hard-to-reach student: For two minutes per day for 10 days in a row, talk with a student about anything they want to discuss.

- Attend extracurricular events when you can fit them in to your schedule to show students you care about their nonacademic pursuits too.

Great Resources

- Cornelius Minor. (2018). *We Got This: Equity, Access, and the Quest to Be Who Our Students Need Us to Be.* Heinemann.

- Dominique Smith, Douglas Fisher, and Nancy Frey. (2020). *Removing Labels, Grades K–12: 40 Techniques to Disrupt Negative Expectations About Students and Schools.* Corwin.

What Should I Keep in Mind About Classroom Management and Student Motivation?

Before we can talk about classroom management, we've got to talk about a common critique of the concept as of 2021. Some have decried popular classroom management philosophies as the micromanagement of student bodies. Before we move on, we must be clear that we do not advocate (or practice) an approach that focuses on micromanaging the bodies of other human beings.

Instead, we're after rightly *stewarding* the learning time we've been given with the students on our rosters.

"Stewardship" is not a common word in today's lexicon, but the idea here is that the classroom we've been given is just that: something we've been given. We've been given it by our employer, we've been given it by our community, and we've been given it by the parents and guardians of the students on our rosters. So then we need to be thoughtful in asking how should this place run, how should it feel, and what outcomes should it have, given that it is a place we have been given responsibility for stewarding.

This returns us to our broader concerns in this chapter around student motivation.

What we want is a classroom space—and let's define that as not just a physical space, but as a social one, an emotional one, and an intellectual one—in which students *want to do work with care and feel that they have all they need to do it*. That's the heart of what classroom stewardship is about. It is about cultivating a space that is safe enough for students to feel they can share their ideas and questions without being mocked or snickered at. It is about making a space where hard work is valued—where it's normal to put forth effort, to ask hard questions, to persist in the face of difficulty. It is about taking care of a space, of time, of a group of people so that student motivation and performance are optimized.

And practically the best methods for stewarding such a space are quite simple. They boil down to three basic steps for nearly everything:

Basic Practical Elements of Effective Classroom Stewardship Approach	Example
Establish behavioral norms (sometimes called agreements or rules or policies or expectations) for your classroom.	We let others finish speaking before we begin speaking ourselves.
Explicitly teach (which can include modeling and discussion) these norms, often at the start of a year and then as needed as the year progresses.	When you've got something you really want to say during a debate that responds to what someone is currently saying, instead of interrupting the other person make a quick note of what you want to say and keep listening to the person. When they've finished, you can respond then.
Establish a standard procedure for responding when the norms are broken.	If someone interrupts another person during an in-class debate, I (the teacher) will politely say, "One at a time."

Once we explicitly lay out these norms and procedures, the final step is simply to make sure to consistently follow them. If we say that no one should raise a hand when another student is talking, like Matt Kay does in his classroom, and some procedure will happen if someone does raise a hand, we need to make sure we stick with that procedure. If we can do that, a great many norms and responses to broken norms can work incredibly well.

Notes

What Is Culturally Responsive Pedagogy, and How Does It Relate to Student Motivation?

Culturally responsive pedagogy (CRP) is essentially about agreeing with the following statements, which we've cited straight from a summary from the Education Alliance at Brown University (n.d.):

- Culture is central to learning.

- Culture plays a role not just in communicating and receiving information but also in shaping thinking processes for individuals and for groups.

- Equitable access to an education isn't possible in settings that don't acknowledge, respond to, and celebrate all cultures.

The gist here is something that's pretty hard to poke a hole in: We need to create learning environments in which all students feel welcomed, valued, and respected, and to do that, we must attend to the many cultural streams that merge together when each of our classes is in session. When we do this, we create ripe conditions for relationships and belonging, all of which fuel student motivation in the ELA classroom.

Thankfully, there is quite a bit of practical guidance available for doing something as big and daunting as culturally responsive teaching. Much of it lies beyond the scope of this book, so we encourage you to read as many of the titles in the Great Resources callouts as possible, then work with your colleagues to ensure you're all incorporating as much CRP into your practice as possible.

For right now, though, try these practices:

- **Actively seek to learn about each student.** A common theme that runs across a great many culturally responsive frameworks is the importance of actively learning about each student. We have already discussed multiple great ways that all teachers can do this, such as Burn 5 and Introductory Letters from Chapter 1 and Tracking Moments of Genuine Connection (earlier in this chapter), but as ELA teachers, we have an additional advantage here because reading and writing are inextricably connected with the personal. Some additional ways to learn more about students while they learn about your ELA subject matter include activities:

  - Start the year with a personal narrative from the students. These narratives are fertile ground to teach important writing concepts such as sentence length variation or word choice, yet they also allow teachers to learn a small slice of the students' stories early in the year.
  - In *Teaching for Joy and Justice*, Linda Christensen reminds us that "we don't build communities *instead* of working on academics. We build communities *while* working on academics" (2009, p. 15, italics added). Specifically, Christensen builds this community early in the year by having students mimic poems that anyone can mimic, such as "Raised by . . ." poems (based off Kelly Norman Ellis's "Raised by Women") and "For

My People" poems (based off Margaret Walker's "For My People"). The students' examples she shares range from serious and touching homages to whimsical and goofy creations ("Raised by Video Games" stands out as the latter), but what they all share is that they tell the teacher a great deal about the student writers and their background.

- Skills are often best worked on in the context of high-interest topics for students. For example, if you are learning about literary devices that add emphasis, such as parallel structure or the purposeful use of dashes, why not have students write a rant about a topic that they want to emphasize while using the devices in the context of their own writing? This is a wonderful way to have them practice a skill while you also learn more about them!

- **Cultivate positive perspectives about parents and families.** If you catch yourself blaming something on a student's home life or complaining about a caregiver interaction, take a minute to reflect on the pieces of the picture you don't possess. Assume, too, that all parents and caregivers love their children and want them to be successful, and remember that many parents did not have a positive experience in school or may not feel a sense of belonging in a school community. In other words, assume good intentions, and keep in mind when talking with parents that you don't know the entire story—or even the half of it!

- **Be a "warm demander."** In our classroom experience, we observe that a leading cause of boredom for students is a course or unit in which too little is expected of them. The idea of high expectations has gotten a messy connotation with many educators of late—for example, so-called "no excuses" charters have been accused of micromanaging student bodies. What we recommend is something older and warmer—specifically, "warm demander" pedagogy. Warm demander pedagogy is an older component of culturally responsive teaching (Kleinfeld, 1975), and seeds of it stretch even further back into research on parenting (Baumrind, 1966). The idea of warm demander pedagogy is that, in a humanized space where relationships are strong, the most effective instructors challenge students to push themselves and grow from dependent to independent learners. High support, high challenge— that's warm demander pedagogy in a nutshell. But when we say "support," we mean cultivating an environment rich in the five key beliefs.

- **Remain curious.** While CRP calls rightly for attending to the cultural backgrounds of students, it's important to remain curious about the cultural backgrounds our students do and don't share. For example, there is not just one single Black culture—there are myriad. There is not just one single Asian American experience—there are many. CRP, when done well, takes a warm, arms-open approach to acknowledging the humanity of all students and delighting in who each of them is.

Great Resources

- Stephanie Smith Budhai and Kristine S. Lewis Grant (Foreword by Matthew R. Kay). (2022). *Culturally Responsive Teaching Online and In Person: An Action Planner for Dynamic Equitable Learning Environments.* Corwin.

- Christopher Emdin. (2016). *For White Teachers Who Teach in the Hood . . . and All the Rest of Y'All Too: Reality Pedagogy and Urban Education (Race, Education, and Democracy).* Beacon Press.

- Zaretta L. Hammond. (2016). *Culturally Responsive Teaching and the Brain: Promoting Authentic Engagement and Rigor Among Culturally and Linguistically Diverse Students.* Corwin.

- Matthew R. Kay. (2018). *Not Light, but Fire: How to Lead Meaningful Race Conversations in the Classroom.* Stenhouse.

- Gholdy Muhammad. (2020). *Cultivating Genius: An Equity Framework for Culturally and Historically Responsive Literacy.* Scholastic Teaching Resources.

MOTIVATION

Notes

What Common Engagement Methods Don't Work as Well as They're Touted?

So far, we've been talking about motivation, not engagement. Sometimes, these terms are used interchangeably, but the literature treats each distinctly.

Engagement is the during-task state in which a student is immersed in a given task. Engagement is super enjoyable, and we should want it for our students wherever possible.

Motivation is the genuine desire in a student to work at a given task with care. In other words, while engagement can get a student *through* a task, motivation can get them *to* the task, *back to* the task (when engagement wanes), or *through* a task that is not engaging for a given student.

We find motivation the superior target—it's more robust and resilient than engagement—and more easily applied to diverse groups of learners. Even still, when increased motivation is paired with increased engagement, the results are all the more powerful.

When it comes to engagement, though, there are a number of widespread suggestions—often ones popularized in social media or created by content creators who haven't been in a classroom this decade—that can range from not particularly effective to downright harmful. Some of these things can potentially work in certain contexts, but overall, we recommend that you don't overrely on them:

Popular Suggestion That We *Don't* Recommend	Instead, Try This
Trying to relate everything in your classroom to something that's hip and current. This is a classic relevance play, and even though it can be really tempting to go this route, we don't recommend it. Here's why: Just because a student is younger than you doesn't mean they're all into the same young-people stuff. For example, relating something to TikTok will resonate with some students but not all of them. Further, knowing and understanding young-person stuff can be hard for any adult, even those recently graduated.	*Frequently speak to the inherent value of the learning that happens in an ELA classroom.* In other words, adopt the view that this classroom isn't something that we need to work to make relevant; instead, what we learn here is fundamentally, *enduringly* relevant. Our task is to make this deeper relevance as clear as we can for each of our students.

Popular Suggestion That We *Don't* Recommend	Instead, Try This
Trying to lead a "pop-up" conversation about every hot-button current event. We understand the urgent desire to pause your planned curriculum and discuss hot-button current events with your students. But this instinct to journey without a map leaves us susceptible to silly or dangerous mistakes. This is when we unintentionally harm kids and/or put them in position to harm each other.	*Incorporate these hot-button current events into your planned curriculum.* If the big moment is important to teach, *teach about it*. Give it the attention and placement in the curriculum that it deserves. In our ELA world, this most often means that we should collect source material in the moment, then use it to supplement texts in our planned curriculum. If it deserves even more attention, design a mini-unit around it.
Doing movie teaching. One of the most common tropes in teacher movies is the teacher standing on their desk to captivate their students. While theatrics have their place in pedagogy, relying on them too often or too flippantly can actually detract from student learning because it becomes about the attention paid to the teacher, not the learning happening inside the minds of the students.	*Doing moving teaching.* Emotions can and should play a role in planning and delivery because they can be powerful tools for engagement, understanding, and retention. But the emotions should be centered on the student, not the teacher. We should seek to surprise students not with our behavior, but in what they discover about themselves or the world. For a student, seeing a strength that they never noticed before or a perspective that they hadn't previously thought about is going to carry far more meaning than the image of a teacher tearing pages out of a book to make a point.
Leading role-play activities without considering all of the consequences. Anecdotally, it sure feels like 90 percent of viral teacher miscues involve role-play activities (e.g., "Imagine you are a slaveholder," or in an example Matt Kay often cites, "Think like a Nazi"). These activities, whether they involve acting or are situated in creative writing, show an incredible lack of foresight. At the very least, they will lead to flare-ups that distract from the intended learning. At the worst, these activities can harm students! And at the extreme end, you can wind up on the local news, having put your administrators in a very tough position defending your choices.	*Use role play thoughtfully.* When using role play, make sure to thoroughly think through the consequences before launching into it. Some things to think about include the following: When do students need to embody the characters in the books they are reading? When would it make more sense to simply design discussion prompts instead? Do students know enough about the identities they are embodying? Or will they be relying upon stereotypes? Is the role play tone deaf? Does it minimize an important perspective? What is the worst possible moment that can result from this role play, and how likely is it to happen, knowing the particular group of students that is participating? Think it all through, and if it seems justifiable—meaning that students will learn the material in a new, engaging way—then, and only then, have at it.

MOTIVATION

HOW CAN I ENSURE THAT MY FEEDBACK AND ASSESSMENT ARE BOTH AS EFFICIENT, EFFECTIVE, AND EQUITABLE AS POSSIBLE?

For generations, feedback and assessment in the ELA classroom almost universally followed certain conventions—conventions so recognizable that they have become clichés, even in the broader culture: copious and often cryptic editorial edits in red pen; runic-looking proofreading marks that can often be looked up on a corresponding sheet; a circled, attention-grabbing grade at the beginning or end as modeled in Figure 1.1.

Figure 3.1

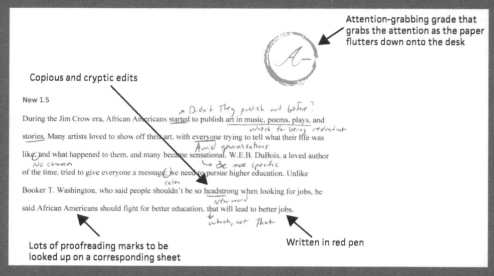

Source: Johnson (2020)

How many papers over your life have looked like this?

Research and evolution of teaching practices have made clear that when it comes to responding to and assessing student work, there is a better way—or, more accurately, many better ways—than following these conventions and acting as what can only be described as a combination of an accountant tallying right and wrong and a copy editor snaking thoughts through the lines and margins (or what we call the Detached Authority).

Yet this approach (or elements of it) persists, likely because it can feel, even to those who know better, both effective and good. While the actual act of learning is silent and invisible, a stack of heavily marked-up papers stands as a tangible monument to the work the teacher has put in. These piles of papers act as firewalls against student/parent/guardian criticism about grades assigned. They are also what many of our beloved mentors did, and to do less can feel like we are cutting corners they never did.

But what makes feedback and assessment effective isn't how many words the teacher writes in the margins (Hattie & Clarke, 2019). What makes feedback effective is how much the student reads, understands, and ultimately learns from it. What makes assessment effective is how accurately you capture the skills and understanding of the student, how clearly that message is passed on to interested audiences, and what impact the assessment has on the student's beliefs about themselves and the class.

This chapter will focus on research-backed and classroom-tested alternatives to the standard, clichéd feedback/assessment convention seen in Figure 3.1—alternatives that in many situations lead to both better instruction and less teacher time spent hunched over student papers on nights and weekends. Here, we'll dig into answering these questions about assessment and feedback:

- ☐ **How are assessment and feedback different?**
- ☐ **What does effective feedback look like?**
- ☐ **How can I manage the paper load and still offer effective feedback?**
- ☐ **How can I ensure that my feedback has the biggest possible impact?**
- ☐ **What role should student self-assessment play?**
- ☐ **What grading options exist for reading and writing classrooms?**
- ☐ **How can I incorporate peer response that actually works?**

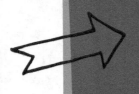

How Are Assessment and Feedback Different?

Across our careers, we have collectively said thousands of times that we were "grading papers" when we were reading and responding to student work. Like the Detached Authority approach to papers, this little snippet of jargon is so common that even non-ELA teachers will likely be familiar with it.

We think that despite its ubiquitousness, it is time to retire the phrase "grading papers" (and also its cousin "marking papers," which is commonly used in countries outside the United States) because when teachers say grading papers they don't generally mean "grading." In many situations, they mean "giving feedback" to student papers, and while this might seem like a semantic hair that is hardly worth splitting, it is worth noting that this conflation of assessment and feedback contributes to one of the most serious and problematic issues when it comes to feedback and assessment: the belief that feedback and assessment usually belong together.

The problem with putting feedback and assessment together is that they are very different activities with different and competing aims:

- **Assessment** is the evaluation of a student's knowledge or skills. It is a photograph, preserving a record of where the student is at that moment for all who are interested. Often, assessment is used to determine a grade for an assignment, although it can also be used to determine next steps for learning.

- **Feedback** is information given to a student, often verbally or through written comments, that is meant to help the student improve. It works best when it focuses on illuminating paths forward.

Feedback and assessment can both offer information about how a student is progressing, but they have different audiences and are looking in different directions. Assessment is a static snapshot of the student's skills at some point in the past for a wide range of parties, while feedback is an aspirational look toward the future specifically for the student—and when the two are combined, these issues tend to follow:

- A grade or other assessment can serve as an indicator to many students that an assignment and the associated learning are done, especially if the grade is within an acceptable range for the student (Belanger & Allingham, 2004).

- When students are ashamed by an assessment, they can avoid the feedback as a defense against further embarrassment (Newkirk, 2017). When students are surprised by an unexpectedly high grade, they tend to bask in the grade while growing disinterested in further growth because they have reached their goals (Belanger & Allingham, 2004).

When feedback and grades are together, feedback tends to focus less on discussing the steps students can take to move forward and spends more time on justifying and explaining the grades to the students, parents/guardians, and administrators who might view them.

Bottom line: When feedback and assessment are combined into the same step, feedback generally loses, which is a major problem because, between the two, feedback is where most of the learning happens.

This is why we suggest finding ways to separate feedback and assessment as often as possible. It is also why we talk about them separately through much of this chapter and throughout this book. When feedback and assessment are separate, each can accomplish its critical job better when it doesn't have the gravity of the other influencing it. We will revisit this idea multiple times in the pages to come, but the following methods are good places to start in decoupling grades and feedback:

- **Try giving feedback-only assignments.** Not every assignment needs a grade that goes into the gradebook. It is all right to focus on feedback while in the process.

- On assessed/graded assignments, **use lots of formative feedback without rubrics** or other scoring/grading in the stages before it is assessed/graded. We'll talk more on how to do this in a time-efficient way in the upcoming sections.

- **Employ a yes/no assessment system around specific learning goals.** In Dave Stuart's class, for example, when students engage in pop-up debate, Dave doesn't assess their performance on a rubric. He sets a baseline expectation for the debate (e.g., each student participates at least one time), and any student that meets this receives that same score in the gradebook. This frees Dave up to provide in-the-moment feedback and coaching to students.

- **Delay the assessment.** Give feedback and assessment to students at different times. We advocate giving the feedback first so that students can process it before the assessment/grade comes in to dominate the conversation.

FEEDBACK

Great Resources

- Kristy Louden. (2017, June 4). Delaying the Grade: How to Get Students to Read Feedback. *Cult of Pedagogy.* https://www.cultofpedagogy.com/delayed-grade/.

- *Teachers Going Gradeless (TG2)* website (www.teachersgoinggradeless.com)

What Does Effective Feedback Look Like?

Disney theme parks are known and somewhat notorious for how closely they manage any moments of interaction between the guest and the park. They call each of these interactions a touchpoint, and their goal is to make each touchpoint—especially the unexpected ones—as easy, fun, and magical as possible. In practice, this means that those standard frustrating amusement park moments, like wandering around the parking lot with exhausted and sunburned children or standing in endless and baking lines, become, at Disneyland, an attendant waiting in the parking lot who can point you right to your car with the scan of a ticket and tents where you can play interactive games as you shuffle forward to the next ride (Disney Institute Blog, 2018).

This idea of touchpoints is a useful way to think about feedback too. Each response to student work—if managed well—can act as a potential moment to strengthen a student's identity, understanding, or relationship with us. How exactly to manage these touchpoints well depends on our students and our classes, but there are a handful of best practices that are nearly universal.

GOOD FEEDBACK IS MANAGEABLE

The traditional Detached Authority approach to providing feedback is not particularly manageable for the teacher or for the students. For the teacher, this role means being responsible for tabulating every error and transcribing every useful thought—a task that can feel akin to the Augean stables when a stack of papers comes in. Taking this approach is a recipe for burnout or getting papers back weeks or months later, even if one consigns nights and weekends to those papers, and it is also worth noting that it is generally not great pedagogy. To understand why, think about why most lessons only have one or two objectives:

Students learn best when they . . .

- Encounter the information multiple times

- Use the information in different ways and combinations over distinctly different learning sessions (Agarwal & Bain, 2019)

- Have time to absorb and process the information

When teachers comment on 10, 15, or 20 distinctly different lessons throughout a paper, the odds are that students simply won't have the time or will to go through the process of revisiting, absorbing, processing, practicing, and ultimately learning all those lessons. Instead, the most likely outcomes are that the students will either get overwhelmed with the sheer amount of information and shut down—which is especially true for the students whose relationships with the subject are the most fraught (Crisp, 2007)—or they will pick a few lessons at random to spend time on, likely forgetting the other topics and creating the same issues the next time.

Further, when a teacher has to make three, four, or five thousand comments (that is what 15 or 20 comments per paper equates to on the scale of all of our students), their only real choice from a time standpoint is to leave those comments really quickly, leading to the cryptic shorthand seen in Figure 3.1—which is far from ideal when it comes to both explaining a writing concept or doing the other things feedback can do, like strengthen relationships with students.

Feedback expert Dylan Wiliam (2018) reminds us that "too much feedback is backwards." Instead, what is far more efficient for us and effective for the students is for the teacher to target one, two, or three things—depending on the needs of the student in that moment—and go deep. This gives the teacher the time and space to fully explain themselves in the feedback (more on that in the next section) and the students the time and space needed to truly learn from teacher feedback. Figure 3.2 offers suggestions on how to prioritize feedback comments.

Figure 3.2 How to Prioritize Feedback Comments

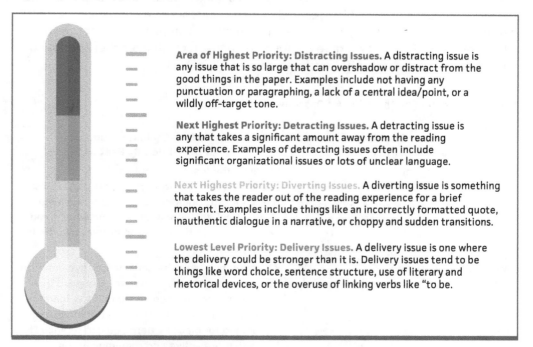

Area of Highest Priority: Distracting Issues. A distracting issue is any issue that is so large that can overshadow or distract from the good things in the paper. Examples include not having any punctuation or paragraphing, a lack of a central idea/point, or a wildly off-target tone.

Next Highest Priority: Detracting Issues. A detracting issue is any that takes a significant amount away from the reading experience. Examples of detracting issues often include significant organizational issues or lots of unclear language.

Next Highest Priority: Diverting Issues. A diverting issue is something that takes the reader out of the reading experience for a brief moment. Examples include things like an incorrectly formatted quote, inauthentic dialogue in a narrative, or choppy and sudden transitions.

Lowest Level Priority: Delivery Issues. A delivery issue is one where the delivery could be stronger than it is. Delivery issues tend to be things like word choice, sentence structure, use of literary and rhetorical devices, or the overuse of linking verbs like "to be."

Source: Adapted from Johnson - *Flash Feedback* (2020)

Keep in Mind

Some ELA Teacher Math

If a teacher marks or comments on 25 little and big issues per paper and has 150 students (which is not that much in this age), that is 3,750 marks/comments. If the teacher takes only 10 seconds per mark/comment (again, this is not that much), that is 10.5 hours needed for the commenting. It is also worth noting that this number doesn't include reading, assessing, or summative notes. The moral of the story? We need to only mark a manageable number of things if we want to have any hope of not spending our nights and weekends marking papers.

GOOD FEEDBACK IS USER-FRIENDLY

In most aspects of our lives, we understand that simply providing our reaction to something is likely to take the constructive out of constructive criticism. A quality soccer coach is unlikely to tell a player simply "You need to score more goals" without any follow-up with how, leaving the player to process the coach's reaction and chart a path forward on their own.

Instead of the traditional Detached Authority response with teacher shorthand on a paper, we suggest using some version of the three-step describe–evaluate–suggest model:

1. The teacher notes a somewhat neutral observation. (Describe)
2. This is followed with a more evaluative statement. (Evaluate)
3. The feedback ends by suggesting a clear path forward. (Suggest)

The objective start can lower defensiveness, a common saboteur of feedback, and the more evaluative part, which can feel to many students as a criticism, is easier to handle because it's instantly followed by potential next steps toward improvement (Hart-Davidson, 2014). See Figure 3.3 for a comparison of what teacher shorthand looks like versus the describe–evaluate–success approach.

Figure 3.3 Teacher Shorthand Versus Describe–Evaluate–Suggest

Teacher Shorthand (aka Teacher Reaction)	Describe–Evaluate–Suggest (aka User-Friendly Feedback)
Needs better organization	I noticed the first paragraph is about _____, and the second paragraph is about _____. As a reader, I struggled to connect the two. What do you think the connection is, and what could you add to help the reader to better make that connection too?
Awkward construction	The sentence uses the verb "to be" five times. In our lesson on linking verbs, we discussed how more active constructions can make writing feel more vibrant and smooth. Using our materials, try looking for places where you can replace "to be" with more active and engaging verbs.
Needs paragraphs	If you take a look, you'll see that there are no paragraph breaks. Modern readers often need these breaks to stay organized, so it would probably be a good idea to include some. You have some say in where you put paragraph breaks, but the most common moments are when you start a new topic, jump in time, or switch speakers in a conversation.

GOOD FEEDBACK IS WISE

In *Culturally Responsive Teaching and The Brain*, Zaretta Hammond (2014, pp. 104–105) discusses the need for "Wise Feedback," which is feedback with the goal of forming a partnership based on the following:

- Honesty about where the student is on a continuum of mastering a skill

- Clear direction about how to move forward

- High standards

- A clear statement on the part of the teacher that they know the student will reach those high standards

Hammond recognizes that feedback, one of the most common and consistent touchpoints between teacher and students, is essential space to do more than just talk about commas and claims. It is also a place for establishing a learning partnership with the student and for helping cultivate a positive reading and writing identity.

This is why we also strive to make sure that feedback

- recognizes the humanity of the student;

- makes clear the humanity and care on the part of the teacher;

- asks a lot of questions and makes space for the teacher to purposefully hear the student;

- weaves high expectations into every word; and

- generally expresses the presence of what David Fuller calls an Interested Reader (Fuller, 1987), or someone who is genuinely curious about the student's writing and the student's growth, as opposed to the Detached Authority, whose job is to separate right from wrong.

How Can I Manage the Paper Load and Still Offer Effective Feedback?

The base task of providing feedback requires that we do three things:

1 Read or look at a piece closely enough to see what is working and what might need work.
2 Track and process our own observations.
3 Craft those observations into responses that meet all the criteria of good feedback.

These necessary steps, when combined with how many students we teach, mean that the task of providing feedback to student work, even when one marks only a manageable amount, is generally measured in hours, not minutes.

So the big question is, *How can teachers provide meaningful feedback while also leading a balanced, sustainable life?* Here are some ways to do that.

DON'T GIVE FEEDBACK TO EVERYTHING

In the same way that teachers often feel compelled to mark every error or issue on a student paper, they also often feel compelled to provide feedback to every piece of student writing, as if their pen is needed to unlock student learning. In these moments, it is worth remembering a common writing instruction maxim: *Students learn and grow more from the act of writing than from reading our responses to their writing.*

While at first it can feel uncomfortable and like breaking a covenant with the students (you write, I read), one of the most important keys for a strong writing classroom is that the teacher doesn't read everything—because reading everything will either mean teachers stay up all night responding to it, will not assign enough writing, or both.

> ### An Important Note on Not Reading All Student Work
>
> In many states, teachers are required by law to report information they have concerning student abuse, self-harm, and violence. And even in states where mandatory reporting laws aren't strong, teachers—and writing teachers in particular—are, in the words of Douglas Fisher and Nancy Frey (2018), the "eyes and ears of the mental health system." For these reasons, it is incredibly important that we are very clear with our students from the beginning about what we will and won't be reading. Being coy about the pieces we will read can open a teacher who doesn't read something that should be reported to legal trouble. Even more importantly, it can lead to missing student admissions of danger—admissions that if students put in writing, they wanted you to see. For more information on mandatory reporting, www.childwelfare.gov has a host of wonderful resources and links.

To know what to read and/or respond to, we use the pyramid of writing priorities (see Figure 3.4). If the purpose is the daily work of processing something, building and practicing skills, or synthesizing thoughts, our general rule is that it is for the students, not us; if we are working on a specific skill, we will often create targeted assignments that receive targeted, flash feedback (see next section) or some form of quick assessment; and every month or so, we will have a larger project or paper that receives more robust feedback and often ends up as a major assessment.

Figure 3.4 Pyramid of Writing Priorities

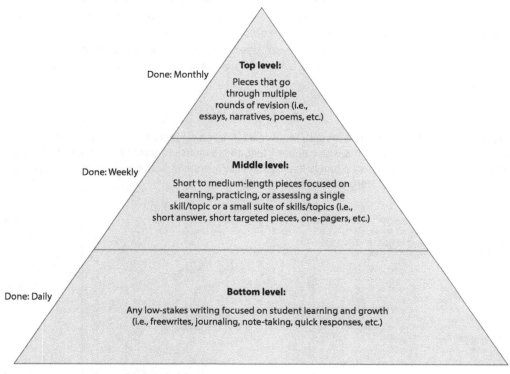

Done: Monthly

Top level:
Pieces that go through multiple rounds of revision (i.e., essays, narratives, poems, etc.)

Done: Weekly

Middle level:
Short to medium-length pieces focused on learning, practicing, or assessing a single skill/topic or a small suite of skills/topics (i.e., short answer, short targeted pieces, one-pagers, etc.)

Done: Daily

Bottom level:
Any low-stakes writing focused on student learning and growth (i.e., freewrites, journaling, note-taking, quick responses, etc.)

Source: Johnson—Flash Feedback (2020)

USE A LOT OF FLASH FEEDBACK

Say the word "feedback," and most people think of comments written through the margins of an essay or story. That is indeed one type of feedback, but it isn't the only type, and it certainly shouldn't be the only feedback students receive because feedback is the most effective when

- it is returned in a timely fashion, and

- students regularly receive it (Fisher et al., 2018, p. 77).

Given the demands of responding to whole papers/projects, even when we are efficient, commenting on larger papers and projects for all of our students generally takes days or even weeks as opposed to hours. It is such a large job that to do it on a regular basis (daily or weekly) simply isn't possible. These demands don't mean that there isn't a place for these larger, more comprehensive comments—there is, and we all use them—but we also supplement them with lots of what we call "flash feedback," or feedback that can be meaningfully offered in a minute or less per student, making it possible to provide regularly and in a timely fashion (often during class). Two of our favorite types of flash feedback are discussed next.

Keep in Mind

Most athletes and creative folks spend many hours practicing on their own before their coach or instructor watches them and offers feedback for the same reasons that we, as teachers, shouldn't read, respond to, and grade everything. Young writers need plenty of practice away from our eyes to maximize their growth.

TARGETED RESPONSE

Targeted response is where students write a piece or do an activity with the goal of building, refining, or demonstrating one or maybe two concepts or skills. By focusing on one or two concepts/skills, the students can put in the time needed to help those new concepts/skills stick, and the teacher can offer a personal, meaningful response quickly because they are only looking for evidence of one or two things. For example, in a craft lesson on repetition, Matt Johnson asks students to write a paragraph (or two) that includes at least two examples of parallel structure, alliteration, and anaphora, and he asks them to annotate each using the comment feature, so he can see that students understand each tool (see the online companion, resources.corwin.com/answersELA, for an example of a flash feedback assignment Matt Johnson uses). Figure 3.5 shows how one recent student completed the assignment, which allowed Matt to see her mastery of the skill quickly.

Figure 3.5 Because the assignment only focuses on three small tools used for rhetorical repetition and the student labeled the usage of each tool, the response to this is easy. A short note can be left on any comment where a tool is misused or misunderstood; if there are no issues, nothing beyond a short, congratulatory statement is needed!

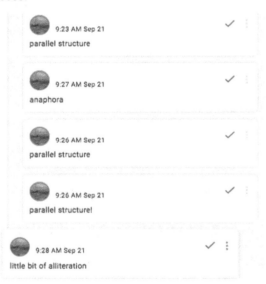

Kiese Laymon's "Da Art of Storytellin' (A Prequel)" is an homage to his grandmother. Please write a homage to someone or something in your life in the box below. When you do, please include at least two examples of parallel structure, alliteration, and anaphora, and please annotate each using the comment feature, so I can see that you understand them. The homage should be a good, solid paragraph, at a minimum.

Last fall I became the mother to a mini rose. It was a rinky-dink, DIY, $5 investment, but I was thoroughly attached. I named her Florence. When her first buds began blooming, little green stalks rising from her pot, I was floored. I created her! I nursed her! I held her hand as her energy was put forth into creating new life. Florence was a darling. I watered her every day, watching her tender roots and making sure she got enough sunlight from my little windowsill. I marveled at every part of her, her little green shoots, her ability to grow with such little material, her bright green color.

She was my closest companion. She watched me grow. She watched me sleep, and read, and become entranced in different shows and movies. She watched me become invested in her, checking on her after school every day, making sure she had enough water, anticipating her sprouts, tending to her every need.

But it became winter, and with winter came nasty weather and straining sunlight. I wasn't sure how to properly care for Florence. Perhaps it was because her "instructions" were nothing more than a how-to on putting the little pellet of dirt into the pot and spreading out her seeds. But Florence became shriveled and dry, her little leaves turning limp and falling off to lie on the dirt resting in her pot. I began to give up on her, considering throwing her out to ease my "will she survive" anxiety.

MICRO-CONFERENCES

A micro-conference is a quick response that is given to a student in person, as opposed to in written feedback. As with targeted response, the secret to keeping these conversations short—one minute or less per student—is to have them focus on a single skill/topic. It is also important to have students do related prep work before the conversation because it enables the students and the teacher to jump right in to the conversation. Figure 3.6 shows an example of a micro-conference focused on writing an introduction.

Figure 3.6 In this micro-conference about writing introductions, students read mentor texts and then answer some questions to prepare for the discussion. Once the students complete the prep work, the teacher can cycle through the room and have short conversations while the students do another task.

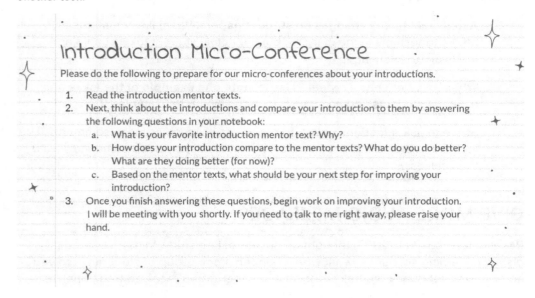

Introduction Micro-Conference

Please do the following to prepare for our micro-conferences about your introductions.

1. Read the introduction mentor texts.
2. Next, think about the introductions and compare your introduction to them by answering the following questions in your notebook:
   a. What is your favorite introduction mentor text? Why?
   b. How does your introduction compare to the mentor texts? What do you do better? What are they doing better (for now)?
   c. Based on the mentor texts, what should be your next step for improving your introduction?
3. Once you finish answering these questions, begin work on improving your introduction. I will be meeting with you shortly. If you need to talk to me right away, please raise your hand.

Great Resources

- Matthew Johnson. (2020). *Flash Feedback: Responding to Student Writing Better and Faster—Without Burning Out.* Corwin.
- Matthew Johnson. (2020, May 10). Flash Feedback: How to Provide More Meaningful Feedback in Less Time [Podcast]. *Cult of Pedagogy.* https://www.cultofpedagogy.com/flash-feedback/.

THE STUDENT SHOULD DO THE WORK

In *Writing Rhetorically*, Jennifer Fletcher (2021) reflects on what she did when she saw students struggling or not turning in assignments when she was a new teacher:

> My solution was to do much of the work for my students. I wrote their introductions for them. I wrote their conclusions for them. I wrote their topic sentences. I even picked a selection of quotations for them to use as support. . . . I thought I was providing scaffolding and modeling, but I wasn't allowing students to make any substantive decisions for themselves. The take-away message was that academic writing is a matter of conformity, not creativity and communication. I was teaching for compliance, not teaching for transfer and agency. (pp. xvii–xx)

In our early years, we also regularly jumped into students' papers and started fixing things and making decisions for them. Like Fletcher, we did this to scaffold and help, but while it often felt productive in the moment because it helped the papers to improve, it didn't offer much to help the students improve their skills. By making the fixes for them, we were, as Fletcher points out, teaching students that writing was about compliance, and we were also robbing them of the opportunity to go through the productive struggle needed to truly grow as writers. In a sense, we were tossing the students a lot of grammatical and rhetorical fish instead of teaching the students how to catch the fish for themselves.

Here are some guidelines to hand over more of the work to students:

- **Avoid making any changes on student papers.** We make comments and offer suggestions in the margins, but the actual student text is theirs and theirs alone to change.

- When a student has a repeated issue, **note one example of the issue** and have the students find and improve upon any future examples.

- **Strive to ask questions or link to resources** as much as make comments. The idea is to illuminate paths forward—paths the students must ultimately walk themselves.

GIVE MORE AUDIO MESSAGES

Researchers Ice et al. (2007) thought up an interesting study. In asynchronous distance learning scenarios, what would happen if one group of students received audio-based feedback on their work while another group received traditional, text-based feedback? Their findings were important.

For one thing, they found that audio feedback improved student satisfaction: Students who received audio feedback were significantly more satisfied with the feedback their teachers gave.

But even more compelling, students who received audio feedback were *three times more likely to apply the contents of audio feedback to subsequent work*. Why did audio feedback have this effect? Here's what the researchers suspect:

- **It conveys nuance.** A written sentence just can't communicate as much as a spoken one can—or at least, it can't communicate as consistently as a spoken one can.

- **It communicates care.** Students in the study reported that they perceived greater care from their instructor, and they cited the audio feedback as the reason.

- **It modified students' view of the importance of what they were doing.** Audio feedback felt more important to students than written feedback—as in, "Wow, this must really be important because my instructor is talking to me about it with his voice, not just his pen."

It is worth noting that this experiment has since been repeated in other settings, and while the effect size isn't always as dramatic, it is often dramatic enough to make a case for making audio feedback a feature of our classes, especially in moments where students need an extra boost of nuance, care, or value. It is also worth noting that audio feedback is generally faster because we can talk faster than we can write, and faster feedback with a bigger effect sounds like a pretty good deal for us!

With today's technology, there are numerous options for leaving audio feedback, but our favorite is the plug-in Mote, which can transcribe, translate, and organize audio messages left for students.

Great Resources

• Dave Stuart Jr. (2020, August 20). How (and Why) to Leave Audio Feedback on Student Work This Year, Whether During In-Person or Distance Learning. https://davestuartjr.com/how-and-why-to-leave-audio-feedback-on-student-work-distance-learning/.

Notes

FEEDBACK

How Can I Ensure That My Feedback Has the Biggest Possible Impact?

While it is debatable whether a tree that falls alone in the woods makes a sound, there is no doubt that feedback unread and unused will not be effective, regardless of how careful, user-friendly, wise, and timely it is. Yet standard practice is returning papers at the end of class, at the end of a unit, never to be spoken of again—which hardly seems a recipe for students to read and internalize feedback.

When feedback is treated like this, a common student response is to glance at it for a few moments before dropping it into the physical or digital recycle bin. Teachers often bemoan this response to feedback, but it is worth asking whether this is the fault of the students or the teachers. If you think about it, the message of fluttering a paper down on the desk without further directions as the bell rings and then never mentioning it again is pretty clear: *The information written in these margins is extra information if you want it. If it were that important, guidance and class time and space would have been given for it.*

As teachers, if we want our feedback—the feedback we likely poured hours into—to make an impact, the first step is that we must make sure that it is read and used. When designing lessons and units, we remember that students need to meaningfully revisit concepts multiple times on multiple days to learn them well, but we often forget this when it comes to feedback. This is likely a time problem, as revisiting feedback multiple times means finding more space in already packed curricula— hardly a simple matter for most busy ELA teachers. Still, it can be done—and in less time—than one might expect, using the following tools:

- **Student-led feedback cycles.** A student-led feedback cycle is built upon the idea that students need to, on average, meaningfully encounter something at least three to five times before it sticks (Hattie & Clarke, 2019). You can do this without displacing a lot of other content by taking what already happens when students draft a piece and weaving feedback into each step. For example, Matt Johnson has long held writing conferences, required significant student revision, used student self-assessment, and asked students to set writing goals with each new unit. So when he created his own student-led feedback cycle, he simply wove feedback into each step along the way. Figure 3.7 shows what that looks like in Matt J.'s classes.

Figure 3.7 A Typical Feedback Cycle in Matt J.'s Classes

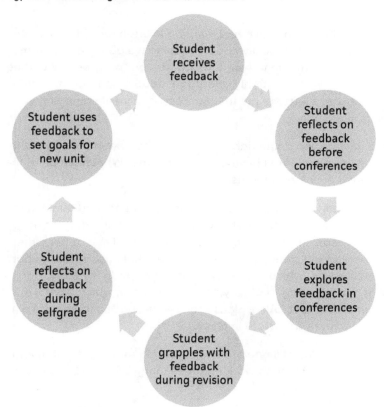

- **Students track the feedback/assessment they receive.** If we ask the students to track their own feedback and assessment throughout a trimester, semester, or year, its impact can be maximized even more. Further, since the students will be the ones doing the work of revisiting and tracking, the additional work for the teacher is minimal. There are multiple ways to do this, but a few effective ones include the following:

  - Have students keep sections in their reading/writing notebooks where they record and track feedback, set goals, and monitor their overall progress (Zerwin, 2020).
  - Students can revisit the feedback and assessments received in regular letters and check-ins throughout the tri/semester, where they share with the teacher how it is going and what they have learned. Figure 3.8 shows an example of a short midsemester letter that has a section devoted to that.

FEEDBACK

Figure 3.8 Midsemester Letter About Revisiting Feedback

Reflection is the fire in which real learning is often forged. When we think closely and critically about anything we do—ranging from basketball to playing piano—we turbocharge our progress. With that in mind, please write a roughly one-page, double-spaced, stream-of-consciousness letter to me that addresses at least some of the following questions:

→ How are you doing right now? What have been the ups of the last quarter? What have been the downs? What have been the major accomplishments?

→ How have you grown in your reading, writing, and thinking skills since the beginning of the course? When doing this, make sure to be specific. For example, don't just say, "I'm a better writer." Instead say something like, "I realized that I used mostly short sentences, which made my writing choppy. In my story, I did a much better job of varying my sentences, which gave it a smoother feel." Also, please reference specific triumphs from the papers you wrote in class.

→ What do you still need to work on as a reader and writer, and how do you plan to work on these things? Please be specific about this too.

→ What feedback have you received that has helped you? What would you like feedback on in the next quarter?

→ What is working well for you in the class? What is not working well, and what can I do to better support you?

● Students can keep a section in their spiral notebooks for the WOOP goals that they set during a semester. (For more on WOOP goals, see Chapter 2.) Dave does this in his classroom (see Figure 3.9 for an example).

Figure 3.9 Student WOOP Example

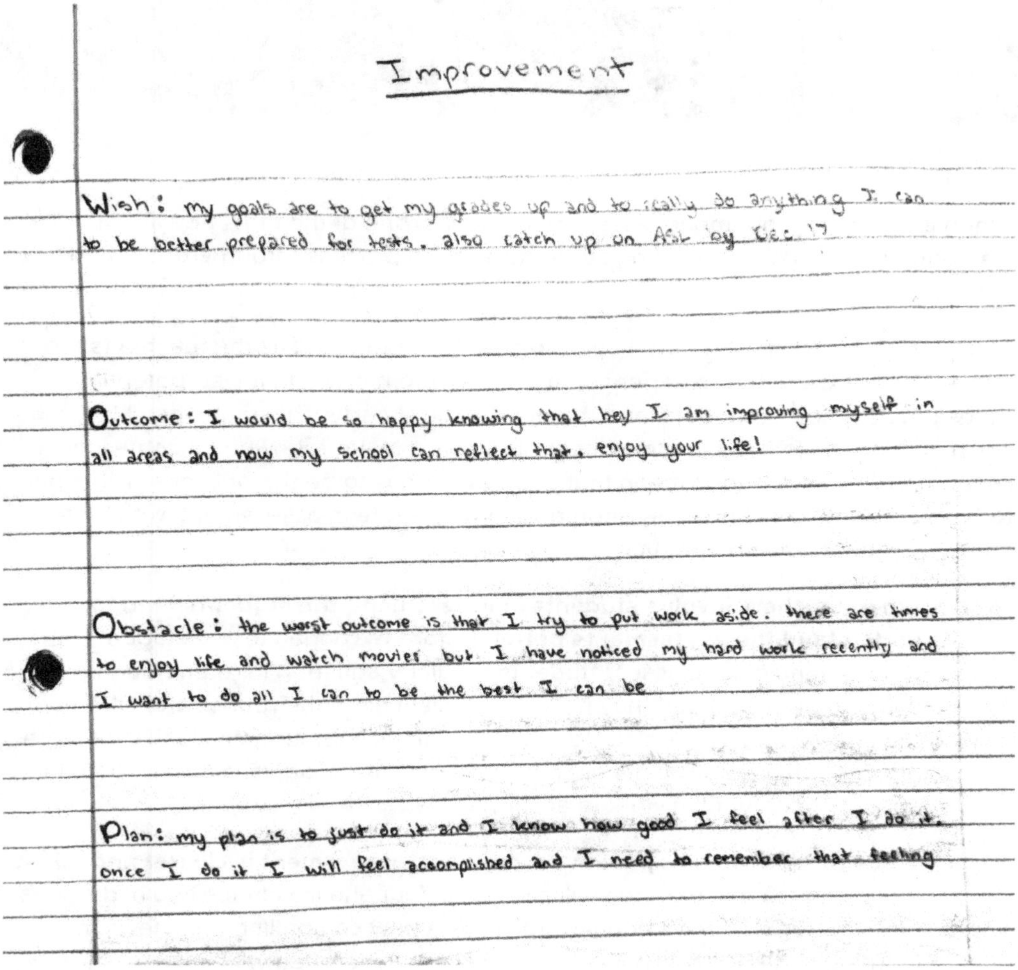

Improvement

Wish: my goals are to get my grades up and to really do anything I can to be better prepared for tests. also catch up on Ask by Dec. 17

Outcome: I would be so happy knowing that hey I am improving myself in all areas and now my school can reflect that. enjoy your life!

Obstacle: the worst outcome is that I try to put work aside. there are times to enjoy life and watch movies but I have noticed my hard work recently and I want to do all I can to be the best I can be

Plan: my plan is to just do it and I know how good I feel after I do it. once I do it I will feel accomplished and I need to remember that feeling

FEEDBACK

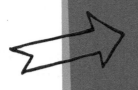

What Role Should Student Self-Assessment Play?

When it comes to high-impact assessment moves, one of the most powerful is also one of the most rare: inviting students into the process through robust and meaningful self-assessment.

Historically, assessment is largely the domain of the teacher, as the teacher is the content area expert, the experienced assessor who has read/viewed potentially thousands of papers/projects, and the more neutral party. These are logical, sensible reasons for why the teacher should play a major role when it comes to assessment, but they don't mean that the teacher has to be the only one with a part to play. Students can, and likely should, also play a role in assessment, which can come with the following benefits:

- **When teachers involve students in assessment, the students tend to understand the assessments better.** Before we began to use student self-assessment in our classes, students regularly admitted (or admitted through the work they did) that they never even glanced at the rubrics and criteria for the assignment. Having students engage in assessment makes this far more unlikely because students must take a close, metacognitive look at both the criteria and their own work to accurately assess it.

- **When students participate in assessment, assessment is clearer and fairer.** While in math two plus two will always be four and in science two hydrogens and an oxygen always equal water, in ELA how compelling one views the opening sentence of a paper will likely vary—and often wildly so—from teacher to teacher. Because the content in an ELA classroom is so subjective and personal, it makes a lot of sense to treat assessment more like a dialogue than a decree because a conversation about the criteria can help to clarify and unpack it for both parties.

- **Partnership during assessment promotes a partnership during the whole writing process.** When a writing process ends with a unilateral grade, it can limit the amount of partnership possible throughout the process because both sides know who will ultimately determine the success of the piece. Having students contribute to the assessment process in a serious way can be a powerful signal of partnership—one that can reverberate throughout the whole process.

- **Student self-assessment can act as a powerful firewall against grade harm.** In middle school, one lower-than-expected grade on one paper led Matt Johnson to largely stop reading and writing for nearly three years. We wish this was an isolated, unusual experience, but sadly, grades and assessment regularly do this type of harm to our students. Inviting students to assess their work first reduces the chance of this happening because the teacher gets to see the students' thought processes and expectations first and use those to calibrate a response.

- **When students do some of the assessment work, teachers can spend less time on assessment and more on feedback and celebration.** Specifically, student self-assessment can free the teacher from the need to write long comments justifying grades and final assessments—comments that can take dozens or even hundreds of teacher hours over the course of a semester and yet tend to lead to far less student growth than formative feedback. Well-trained students can be strikingly effective in assessing and offering the justification (see Figure 3.10), freeing the teacher to focus time on things like giving more formative feedback, celebrating student successes at the end of a unit, and adding more balance to one's life and teaching practice.

Figure 3.10 Examples of Student Self-Assessment

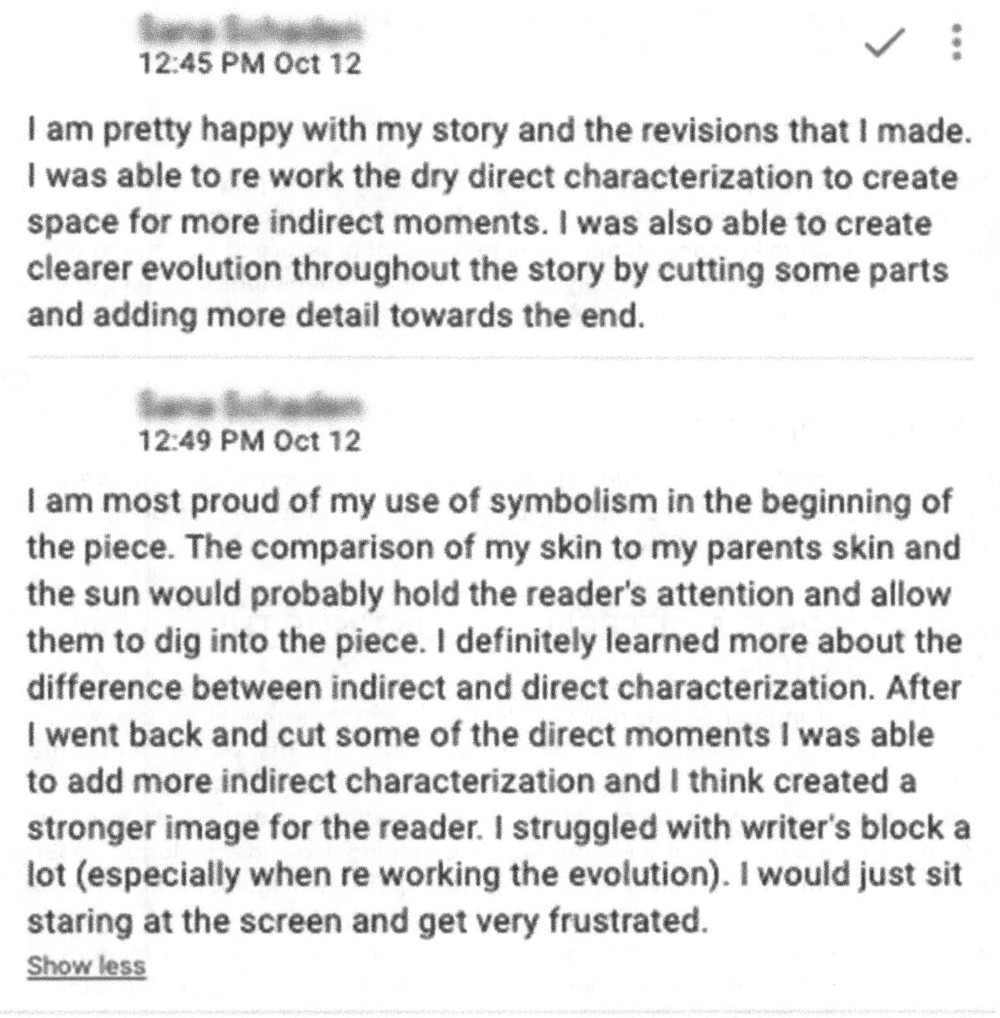

12:45 PM Oct 12

I am pretty happy with my story and the revisions that I made. I was able to re work the dry direct characterization to create space for more indirect moments. I was also able to create clearer evolution throughout the story by cutting some parts and adding more detail towards the end.

12:49 PM Oct 12

I am most proud of my use of symbolism in the beginning of the piece. The comparison of my skin to my parents skin and the sun would probably hold the reader's attention and allow them to dig into the piece. I definitely learned more about the difference between indirect and direct characterization. After I went back and cut some of the direct moments I was able to add more indirect characterization and I think created a stronger image for the reader. I struggled with writer's block a lot (especially when re working the evolution). I would just sit staring at the screen and get very frustrated.

Show less

When it comes to student self-assessment, there are a few keys that help to make it meaningful.

THE CRITERIA NEED TO BE CLEAR

Many students don't regularly look at standards and assignment criteria, and the standards/criteria we must often use are not exactly student-friendly. Before students can accurately assess, they need to have a clear understanding of what the standards/criteria mean. Some ways to encourage this clarity include the following:

- Co-constructing assignment rubrics with students where you unpack standards/criteria and translate them into more student-friendly rubrics for class use

- Norming student understanding of the criteria by using a wide variety of different mentor texts

- Modeling assessment before students engage in it

- Engaging in practice assessment, where students practice assessing themselves before the final assessment

THE STUDENTS LEAD

It is best to have students start the conversation and teachers play the role of responder. Because of the historically unequal roles of teacher and student, as soon as a teacher talks many students will feel instant pressure to agree with the teacher's stance, even if they actually disagree with it. When students assess first, though, they can present their thoughts without the heavy influence of the teacher pushing on the scale.

ASK FOR EVIDENCE

Much like a student essay inevitably goes deeper when evidence gets involved, student assessments tend to be more thoughtful and accurate when students must justify their scores with evidence.

WHEN THERE IS A DIFFERENCE, CONTINUE THE CONVERSATION

Given the wide range of parties that will view and use assessments, we believe that it is important that the teacher agree with student assessments. We strive to settle disagreements by having a conference where we try opening a dialogue about the gap between our assessments. In these conversations, as with assessment, let students lead and try to hear them out before engaging in a wider dialogue about the disagreement. These conversations are often quite illuminating for both parties, and the result—whether it is students redoing the assignment to get the score they want or the teacher offering an alternative score—often acts as a firmer foundation upon which the students and teacher can move forward in the pursuit of helping them to grow their skills.

What Grading Options Exist for Reading and Writing Classrooms?

Many thoughtful educators in recent years have advocated for many thoughtful but different positions about grading, but there is one thread that tends to unite these disparate arguments: Grades are indeed problematic. A long history of scholarship points to the fact that in many cases grades can interfere with learning, decrease intrinsic motivation, and push our students into a range of less-than-desirable behaviors ranging from avoiding risks to plagiarism (Blackwelder, 2020, p. 46). Further, grades are often inaccurate and imprecise. After all, how can a single letter or number capture the totality of a student's work, understanding, and skills? And what work and skills should contribute to the grade? And in what percentages?

These issues with grades are real, and in an ideal world, maybe they would mean that we wouldn't have to ever rely on a series of numbers or letters to capture who a student is and the skills they possess. But in the schools and systems we occupy, it isn't that easy. The use of grades or the type of grade used often isn't a teacher choice but a matter of contractual obligation. Further, grades exist in part because of a wide variety of parties and factors: Parents/guardians, administration, special education or ELL services, colleges and universities, and potential employers all need information about students, and the loads many teachers carry prohibit the ability to write long narratives about every student for every audience. Further, while we hate to admit it, not every student will value and be intrinsically motivated to do everything we do in our classrooms, and extrinsic rewards can be effective for getting students to do tasks that they don't value. Of course, by tying a task to an extrinsic reward, it makes it less likely a student will value it in the future, and given what a blunt and potentially imprecise instrument grades can be, the information the other parties receive from them might be minimally useful or even misleading. You can see how quickly discussion of grades gets messy, and that is before we even get into related topics like the use of rubrics; whether letters, numbers, standards, or nothing is the best system; what to do with extra credit and late work; and if factors like effort, improvement, or behavior should factor into a grade.

This is all to say that grading is complicated, and while pursuing the best practices possible is important, we aren't sure there is one best practice for all students and classrooms. Instead, each potential system offers its own pros and cons, and for many classes, an amalgamation of two or more might make the most sense. With that caveat, here are some of the most commonly used grading/assessment systems in ELA classrooms and potential pluses and minuses for each.

POINTS-BASED

Likely the most commonly used system, a points-based approach is where a teacher assigns a point value to some/all of the work done in class. The students then receive points on each assignment based on performance, and at the end of the marking period, the points are added up and converted into a grade, usually one based on percentages.

Potential Pros	Potential Cons
→ Being the most common grading system, it is generally well understood by students and others who view the grades. → It is also—from a statistical perspective—likely the clearest and most straightforward. → It provides a fair amount of teacher autonomy to adjust the curriculum based on what students need.	→ While this approach makes it clear how much work a student needs to do to get a certain grade, what each grade means can be at times unclear because the assignments are not necessarily connected to standards. → It can be inconsistent across classes, as what leads to certain points in one class can be totally different than what leads to points in another class. → Points-based approaches often give the appearance of objectivity, which can shut down conversation about assessment because it establishes the teacher as the lone keeper of grades.

STANDARDS-BASED

In standards-based grading, the grade is based on a student mastering a list of skills and content. The scores connected to these skills/content then generally convert into a grade.

Potential Pros	Potential Cons
→ The skills/content that factor into the grade are often clearer than in a straight point system. → This approach often allows for more flexible pacing. When students quickly display mastery of a certain skill/content, a standards-based approach can allow them to jump right to a skill/content they haven't mastered yet. → It can complicate the picture for students in a good way. For example, instead of a student simply seeing themselves as a C-plus or A-minus writer, they can see how they each have areas they are strong in and areas in need of improvement.	→ As with a rubric, standards can lock a teacher into focusing on certain topics, potentially limiting autonomy and personalization in regard to other topics. → It is not always easy to include some factors that are important to some teachers, such as effort or growth. → As with points, standards can potentially put a veneer of objectiveness on something that is still deeply subjective.

What Is Mastery-Based Instruction?

Mastery-based instruction is a derivative of standards-based grading where students don't move on to the next skill or concept until they have mastered the previous one. The idea is to try and eliminate gaps while also allowing students to move at the pace that is best for them.

CONTRACT-BASED

A sort of mirror opposite of standards-based grading, labor/contract-based assessment operates according to the notion that all assessment systems and standards, being created by humans, are inherently subjective and biased. Thus, without some impartial judge to arbitrate, the fairest way to grade in an ELA class is to either base it upon the work put in by students or to determine (with student input and agreement) some set of criteria for how the class will be graded that gets captured in a grading contract.

Potential Pros	Potential Cons
→ It eliminates, or at least allows one to process, potential biases in standards and grades. → Growth and effort, which are often some of the main components of the grade, are prioritized. → If done well, it can provide a clear path to success, one that potentially feels within the reach of all students.	→ It can be hard to sync it with school/district/state standards. → It can cap effort once students have reached the threshold for the grade they want. → It can deprioritize skills and content that might help students in the future.

CONFERENCE/SELF-EVALUATION-BASED

In a conference- or self-evaluation-based classroom, the students and the teacher determine the grades through self-evaluation conferences at the end of papers/projects/units/marking periods. In the best examples, data from the unit or paper being graded (scores on reading quizzes/tests, effort and work completed, standards met, etc.) is generally used as the foundation for these evaluations and conferences.

Potential Pros	Potential Cons
→ It humanizes the grading process by turning it into a conversation. → It invites the students to be active agents in their own assessment, potentially increasing buy-in and understanding. → It allows for increased flexibility.	→ Having conversations long enough to be meaningful can take a lot of class time. → While well-trained students are generally harder on themselves than most teachers are, real conversation can lead to possible disagreement, which can be hard to resolve, given the importance of grades for many students. → The increased flexibility can lead to a muddying of what the grade means.

TRULY GRADELESS CLASSROOMS

Given the negatives that come with grades, some classes, schools, and even systems (e.g., Montessori or Rudolph Steiner) don't use any grades at all. Instead, these systems often offer short narratives explaining the development of the student.

Potential Pros	Potential Cons
→ It eliminates many of the negatives that can come with grades. → It lessens the chances of students being placed into boxes that can be hard to escape from. → It allows the teacher to focus on feedback, which is where growth happens.	→ It is not possible in many traditional contexts, given the time-consuming nature of narratives and the classloads teachers carry. → Having no specific standards can potentially lead to gaps or dramatically different experiences and content from class to class. → Narratives can be hard for some stakeholders too. For example, many colleges might not have a good way to weigh a narrative versus more traditional measures like GPAs.

Great Resources

If you are interested in going deeper into any or all of these assessment models, here are some titles worth pursuing:

- Jane Danielewicz and Peter Elbow. (2008). A Unilateral Grading Contract to Improve Learning and Teaching. *College Composition and Communication, 61*(2), 244–268.

- Kareem Farah. (2021, March 7). How to Set Up Mastery-Based Grading in Your Classroom. *Cult of Pedagogy.* https://www.cultofpedagogy.com/mastery-based-grading/.

- Joe Feldman. (2018). *Grading for Equity: What It Is, Why It Matters, and How It Can Transform Schools and Classrooms.* Corwin.

- Alfie Kohn. (2020). *Ungrading: Why Rating Students Undermines Learning (and What to Do Instead*; Susan D. Blum, Ed.). West University Press.

- Starr Sackstein. (2015). *Hacking Assessment: 10 Ways to Go Gradeless in a Traditional Grades School.* Times 10 Publishing.

- Sarah M. Zerwin. (2020). *Point-Less: An English Teacher's Guide to More Meaningful Grading.* Heinemann.

OTHER GRADING/ASSESSMENT CONSIDERATIONS

Alongside these larger systemic choices, there are other considerations to keep in mind when it comes to grading and assessment. And while the three of us don't use the exact same approach to grading/assessment, we do tend to agree on the following principles:

- **Grades and assessment should be openly discussed with students**. As young teachers, some of us used to make it clear to our students that grades were not up for debate. Looking back on it, we realize now that this stance where the grade was a closely guarded secret recipe held by the teacher—while meant to show strength—was a sign of insecurity. Whatever the system or blend of systems that the teacher uses, dialoguing around it with students will likely make it clearer and easier to use for them and clearer and more comfortable for the teacher to use.

- **Late work should be accepted.** In *Grading for Equity*, Joe Feldman (2019) claims that not penalizing late work generally does not lead to more late work and can sometimes lead to less late work (p. 116). Matt Johnson was somewhat skeptical of this claim when he first read it, but when he made the jump to no grade penalty for late work during the Covid-19 pandemic, this is exactly what happened in his classroom, and it has been happening ever since. Matt Kay does dock a couple of points for late work but always accepts it and gives students access to a good-enough grade (in his school, that's a B).

- **There needs to be space for do-overs.** If learning is the purpose of the classroom, allow space for students to revise or resubmit assignments (big or small) for a higher grade. Our hesitation with this used to be that our paper loads were already bordering on unsustainable and adding another possible stack of do-over papers might be the proverbial needle that would cause these camels to collapse. These days though, digital revision and version history tools allow teachers to almost instantly see the specific changes a student made, and if the students are self-assessing, the reassessment can go even faster. This means that there is almost no time penalty on the part of the teacher for allowing revised/resubmitted drafts, yet the payoff for students can be significant.

- **Seek out and create sanctuaries from grades.** Whatever the assessment/grading structure, there are some processes where grades/assessments don't interfere with the learning happening in class:

  - The first weeks of class, where the focus is on building skills, routines, and community, not getting points or checking off a bunch of standards
  - The early drafts of papers and projects, where the focus is on feedback, not assessment
  - Specific activities in class that don't need assessment—for example, our choice reading has no grades or assessment beyond occasional check-in conferences because the purpose is to get students to grow as readers or grow into readers, and a grade/score would likely only interfere in doing that

AN IMPORTANT NOTE ABOUT GRADES AND ASSESSMENT

Grading and assessment are among the most controversial topics within education because a discussion about grades and assessment is a proxy discussion for what we value, believe school to be about, and what skills we believe the next generation needs to go forward into a brave new world. When deciding what grading and/or assessment approach or blend of approaches works for you, we encourage you to weigh the answers to the following questions:

- What are you required to do by your school/district?

- What does flourishing and success in your classroom look like to you?

- What skills and content are key to success in your class?

- What potential pros would be the most positive for your students, and what potential cons would be the most negative for your students?

Use your responses to triangulate the approach that might work best for you. Then, each year, go back to the drawing board and repeat this examination with your experiences from the previous year in the pursuit of how to do it even better the next time.

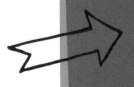

How Can I Incorporate Peer Response That Actually Works?

Any conversation about peer response in the classroom should probably start with understanding that, for many students, peer response is a unique constellation of discomfort and terror, in part because of the following reasons:

- **The act of peer response is in part an act of taking a close look at one's deficiencies.** While the importance of that might be intellectually clear, it is still often unpleasant and embarrassing. Others aren't always kind concerning the areas where we need improvement.

- **Peer response is public.** Normal decorum has long been for teachers to return big tests and papers facedown to avoid shaming some students by broadcasting what they need to work on. Still, that is exactly what peer response is built around: exposing a student's errors and overall position along a learning continuum for others to see.

- **Students often feel unqualified to do peer response.** Many students feel unprepared for the job of assessing someone else's writing and view other students as being equally unprepared to meaningfully assess their work. This is likely due in large part to steady messaging that many students receive in our educational system that the teacher is the expert of all in the room while the students are the perennial novices in training.

- **Did we mention that peer response is so public?** The classic structure of peer response is for the reviewer to sit right next to the reviewee. Even many of the most accomplished writers we know often noticeably squirm when someone looks at their work in their presence, so one can imagine how many of our students feel.

Add these things together, and peer response can be a minefield of social and intellectual risks, one that must be cleared before many students will actively engage in it in a meaningful way. To do that, we approach peer response like this:

REFRAME IT

Many students will come into class with disinterest or antipathy toward peer response borne from negative peer response experiences in the past. This is a major problem because, for peer response to be effective, students need to believe in its value (Chapter 2). With that in mind, it is a good idea to do the following before engaging in peer response:

- Make clear what peer response is (an opportunity for meaningful discourse around writing) and is not (just a live and more error-prone version of spelling/ grammar check).

- Air out feelings by openly discussing what has made peer review ineffective in the past and what might make it work in the future.

- Make a case for why peer response matters.

- Normalize and celebrate errors and rough first drafts in advance. Scan the QR for a useful presentation from Ta-Nehisi Coates to a group of high schoolers.

Ta-Nehisi Coates presents on *We Were Eight Years in Power: An American Tragedy*

Why Peer Response Is Important

1. When students know how to respond as peers, they can be remarkably effective, allowing for exponentially more quality feedback in the classroom.

2. The act of responding to another's paper actually makes the reviewer's own writing better, especially on a similar assignment, because looking at the work of someone else with a critical eye prompts us to be more critical with our own work (Cho & Cho, 2011).

3. Other students' papers are the ultimate mentor texts. What they do and don't do can help to teach us what to do and not do.

TEACH IT

Peer response is often seen as a natural, straightforward thing, but quality peer response is anything but. When students meaningfully engage with one another, they are engaging in two difficult things simultaneously: writing instruction and managing social interaction. So we teach students about best practices in both areas in the way that a writing center would train student mentors to interact with those who visit. During this "training," it's useful to practice on a wide variety of papers. Although this does take time, these training papers act as mentor texts, and critiquing them together helps to train students in how they can better and more metacognitively approach their own papers.

Figure 3.11 provides key concepts we introduce to students before engaging in peer response; you can find a downloadable version of this in the online companion, resources.corwin.com/answersELA.

Keep in Mind

Consider micro peer responses, where students look at small sections of each other's work (like introductions, theses, conclusions, etc.); peer response on smaller and more targeted assignments; or anonymous peer response, where students exchange papers with aliases in the place of their names (they often have fun constructing these).

Figure 3.11 Peer Response 101

A successful peer response often shares these characteristics:

It focuses on key things.

The human brain can only absorb so many new things at once. When you review, don't try to focus on everything. That is called proofreading, and it comes later in the process when there are fewer things to grapple with. Instead, focus only on a handful of key issues, and make them big ones!

It is human.

The best reviewers don't treat peer review like a game of whack-a-mole for errors. They instead respond in a warm and welcoming way that lets the reader know that a human being is on the other end. Also, they offer positive and specific praise along with the moments of constructive criticism.

It is specific.

Telling a partner that a paper is "good" or "needs better flow" is not very helpful because those statements are far too broad. The best reviews are specific and precise. They offer suggestions such as "The last four sentences were short; try making at least one of them longer."

It doesn't try to give all the answers.

Your job as a peer responder is not to fix everything. It is to offer the author a reader's perspective. With that in mind, don't feel like you need to always give answers. Often, a question or statement of how you experienced something can be more powerful and useful than doing the author's work for them.

It trusts itself.

You might not be an English teacher, but you know when things sound wrong, when you are confused by the organization, and when you are interested/persuaded or not. Trust that your observations are valid and worthwhile, and they will be!

Great Resources

- Young Hoan Cho and Kwangsu Cho. (2011). Peer Reviewers Learn From Giving Comments. *Instructional Science, 31*(5), 629–643. https://www.jstor.org/stable/23882823.

- Emily Esfahani Smith. (2015, April 23). Mixed Signals: Why People Misunderstand Each Other. *The Atlantic*. https://www.theatlantic.com/health/archive/2015/04/mixed-signals-why-people-misunderstand-each-other/391053/.

- Nick Stockton. (2014). What's Up With That? Why It's So Hard to Catch Your Own Typos. *Wired*. https://www.wired.com/2014/08/wuwt-typos/.

STRUCTURE IT THOUGHTFULLY

In order to make peer response as smooth and meaningful as possible, it can be helpful to use various structures. The following are some of the most important:

- **Provide protocols for newer reviewers.** These lay out exactly what steps to take and what to look for while also leaving space for students to authentically respond. Figure 3.12 provides an example.

- **Group students carefully.** Doing peer response in groups of three can often take pressure off each individual student and limit the impact when a student doesn't fully engage. Further, it might even be worth letting students choose partners initially to help students feel most comfortable.

- **Incorporate community building.** Having students connect over something before peer response in an effort to build community and camaraderie can often allow students the comfort to get to the deeper, more meaningful work faster.

- **Listen to student needs.** For some students, peer response is truly terrifying. By creating opportunities for students to express those worries ahead of time (like with a Google Form the day before that asks for grouping/peer response needs, questions, or worries) and then problem-solving around concerns thoughtfully, you can increase the likelihood that even if the student isn't fully ready to engage yet, they will likely get there soon.

Figure 3.12 Example of Peer Response Protocol

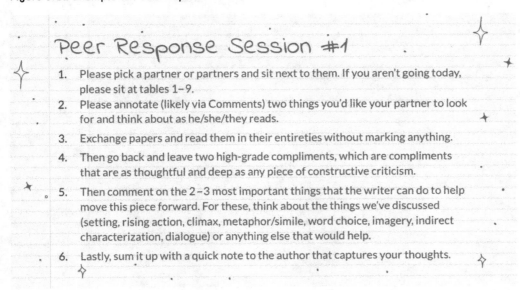

Peer Response Session #1

1. Please pick a partner or partners and sit next to them. If you aren't going today, please sit at tables 1–9.
2. Please annotate (likely via Comments) two things you'd like your partner to look for and think about as he/she/they reads.
3. Exchange papers and read them in their entireties without marking anything.
4. Then go back and leave two high-grade compliments, which are compliments that are as thoughtful and deep as any piece of constructive criticism.
5. Then comment on the 2–3 most important things that the writer can do to help move this piece forward. For these, think about the things we've discussed (setting, rising action, climax, metaphor/simile, word choice, imagery, indirect characterization, dialogue) or anything else that would help.
6. Lastly, sum it up with a quick note to the author that captures your thoughts.

GRADUALLY RELEASE AS NEEDED

As students grow in their understanding of and comfort with peer response, start to take away the frames and let the students, with occasional reminders, engage in more and more organic and self-directed sessions. The specific moment to start releasing will depend on the class and the students, but you will know it when you see it!

chapter FOUR

WHAT DOES STRONG ELA INSTRUCTION LOOK LIKE?

Few disciplines are more widely (and easily) caricatured than English language arts. Matt Kay thinks of the multiple parodies of *Dead Poets Society* or the recurring "Poetry Club" sketches on *Saturday Night Live*. It's to be expected, with all of the emotion inherent in the content we teach, the often melodramatic nature of teenage writing, and the popular (and meme-able) theatric pedagogical moves used to keep kids attention. It's mostly all in good fun (Matt Kay chuckles every year when students show him the viral TikTok of a "teacher" strenuously overanalyzing *Lord of the Flies*), but it is not entirely harmless—especially when these same critiques are co-opted by those eager to roll their eyes at (and actively undermine) anything student-centered or "less traditional."

This all begs these questions: Where is the line between good pedagogy and the stuff that is rightly parodied or criticized? What moves don't just "look good" but actually help kids become better readers, writers, and communicators? What innovations contribute to the field, and which ones distract us? And what moves, ultimately, are more about *us* than helping our students to flourish?

The number of answers and conflicting answers to these questions about quality instruction can be overwhelming for today's ELA teachers, especially with the emotional weight that many carry in the post-2020 world. Chapter 4 seeks to sift through the pile of messages (and mixed messages) to uncover what strong, effective, student-centered instruction actually looks like—and what practical steps we can take to get there. We'll answer these questions throughout this chapter:

- ☐ **What are mirrors and windows, and why do students need both?**
- ☐ **How can I best teach critical thinking?**
- ☐ **What is metacognition, and why is it so important?**
- ☐ **How much choice and voice should students have?**

- [ ] What are the essentials of an impactful reading/writing conference?
- [ ] How can I do direct instruction well? (What should be done with the lecture?)
- [ ] What is project-based learning (PBL), and how does it fit with a reading and writing classroom?
- [ ] How do we help our students remember things?
- [ ] How can mentor texts be used to accelerate writing skills?
- [ ] What role can emotions (surprise, uncertainty, joy, anger) play in instruction?

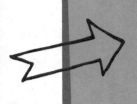

What Are Mirrors and Windows, and Why Do Students Need Both?

Dr. Rudine Sims Bishop famously crafted the analogy of "Mirrors, Windows, and Sliding Glass Doors" in her 1990 essay. A text behaves as a "mirror" when it reflects aspects of a student's own cultures, while a text acts as a "window" when it allows students to interact with other cultures. This analogy's simplest and most applied lesson is that students of color deserve to see themselves in the books we teach. There can be no doubt about this. The second lesson is that students who are privileged to always see themselves in more "common" class texts might, as Bishop argued in a 2015 interview, "get an exaggerated sense of their own self-worth, and a false sense of what the world is like" so they would benefit from a window into other people's stories. (You can view that interview by scanning the QR code in the margin.)

Rudine Sims Bishop interview

Both are true. *But there are a few underapplied lessons:*

- **Underrepresented students *need* "window" narratives too.** Not just into dominant cultures, as per usual, but into stories that engage *other* underrepresented cultures. Black students, for instance, need to read about authentic Asian characters, not just for their intellectual benefit but because in many of the communities our students come from, the real-life relationships between these groups are as rich and complex as more commonly addressed Black/white relationships.

- **Students from dominant cultures *need* "mirror" narratives too. But clean mirrors.** Not the funhouse mirrors that distort their culture to make it perfect. Offer a range of stories that expose complexity and acknowledge white supremacy when applicable. When teaching *Lord of the Flies*, for instance, one can thoughtfully discuss why William Golding (1954, p. 180) uses caricatures of Indigenous peoples to show how the boys become more "savage." When the boys act up, why does Piggy shout, "Which is better—to be a pack of painted Indians like you are, or to be sensible like Ralph is?" Why is *that* the analogy that Golding goes to in that scene?

- **Disaggregate whiteness.** Read and discuss Irish stories, Italian stories, Jewish stories, and the like while emphasizing and discussing specific cultural elements.

- **Disaggregate people of color.** Teach Latinx stories from specific Latinx cultures, emphasizing and discussing specific cultural elements. Do the same with all disparate cultures that are often lumped into one group.

- **Disaggregate gender and sexuality.** Teach stories where LGBTQ+ characters are complex, round characters.

All of this is especially important given the present-day reemergence of racist fearmongering and the eagerness among some parents and communities to censor certain voices. We need to normalize this approach to text selection whenever we get the chance to get new books, and we must definitely keep it in mind when selecting supplementary texts.

Great Resources

- #DisruptTexts: social media hashtag

- Afrika Afeni Mills. (2022). *Open Windows, Open Minds: Developing Antiracist, Pro-human Students.* Corwin.

- Gholdy Muhammad. (2020). *Cultivating Genius: An Equity Framework for Culturally and Historically Responsive Literacy.* Scholastic Teaching Resources.

Notes

What Are Mirrors and Windows, and Why Do Students Need Both?

93

How Can I Best Teach Critical Thinking?

"Critical thinking" is a problematically overextended term. It's a term like "close reading"—we can all agree we want kids to be great at it, but if you put 10 random educators in a room and have them each write down their clearest, most actionable definition of close reading, you'd get a wide range of meanings.

Daniel Willingham, a cognitive scientist who writes for educators, says that cognitive science sees critical thinking as "a subset of three types of thinking: reasoning, making judgments and decisions, and problem-solving" (2007, p. 11). In other words, even though we frequently reason, make decisions and judgments, and solve problems, these aren't always done in a critical manner.

The trouble here is that, even though Willingham's treatment of the term is among the clearest, most robust, and most concise that you'll find, it still feels overwhelming for us as teachers. We see the Willingham definition and read his article, and think, "OK—someday I'd like to have my head fully wrapped around that and to have a solid plan for attending to it in all of my courses." But in terms of the practical—the "What do I do tomorrow?"—critical thinking leaves us at a loss.

This is why in *These 6 Things* Dave Stuart (2018) recommends focusing on argumentation instead. When we place argumentation up against Willingham's definition of critical thinking, we find it to be at least a component of effective problem-solving, it definitely requires reasoning, and it's central to making sound judgments and decisions.

So even though "argument" isn't synonymous with "critical thinking," teaching our students how to argue and giving them repeated opportunities to practice can do a good job of giving our students critical thinking practice. At the core of critical thinking, we believe, is argument, and this distinction helps us breathe a little easier.

With that said, not all argumentative classwork is created equal. Try these to make arguments better in your room:

- **Define arguments as something way better than zero-sum.** Dave calls the kinds of arguments he's after in his classroom "earnest and amicable." Everyone's working hard to get to the bottom of a question, to hold their views loosely, to bring and weigh evidence—that's the earnest part. And everyone's doing it in a mutually respectful fashion, with the aim of walking away from the conversation as better and wiser friends—that's the amicable.

- **Work to cultivate a culture of earnest and amicable argument.** The thing with definitions like those discussed in the previous paragraph is that they don't magically become culture once you state them to the class or post them on your wall. Such life-giving argumentative cultures are built one debate at a time, one bit of teacher feedback at a time, one celebrated moment of student brilliance or grace or dignity at a time. Cultures are formed much the way gardens are: day by day, act by act.

Share lots of argument examples (and maybe use Essay/Argument of the Week). A great many students believe that what defines an essay is how many paragraphs it has (five) and whether it resembles a hamburger in its construction. While we think there is potentially a place for this form in some classrooms, it is only one small fraction of argumentative/essay writing. One way to show the various approaches to argument in writing is to share regular, varied examples of argumentative essay writing. In his classes, Matt Johnson does this through his "Essay of the Week," which is an argument-focused version of Kelly Gallagher's well-known "Article of the Week" (2009). The class unpacks another, different essay or argument each week in order to see the possibilities that exist within argumentation. (View the QR codes in the margin for Matt Johnson's Essay of the Week program and how to make it work in your classroom, Kelly Gallagher's list and archive of Articles of the Week, and Dave Stuart's collection of Articles of the Week, where he links to his journey as an educator using these in class.)

Matt Johnson's Essay of the Week post

Provide generous amounts of knowledge-building work. Dave Stuart recounts the day he had his students debate about how the United States should respond to North Korea's latest missile test (after they had read a brief article about it). The debate was embarrassing; after the third student said something to the effect of "We should nuke them," Dave shut it down, telling his students that they'd try the debate again in a few weeks. Over the course of those few weeks, Dave didn't give any instruction on North Korea; he just provided his students with a series of articles on the North Korean situation that included the topics of human rights abuses, connections to the Korean War, and the relationship with China. One day, Dave told his students that they'd again be having the North Korea debate, and guess what? Not a single student suggested barbarism. Instead, students suggested a variety of humane solutions to the complex crisis. The cause for this burst in critical thinking? Knowledge—something that, while it can look like the opposite of opinion, is generally a prerequisite for thoughtful opinions.

Kelly Gallagher's Article of the Week resources

Dave Stuart's Article of the Week collection

Great resources

Here are some of our favorite places to find arguments to share with the class:

- The *New York Times* Learning Network, which has regular student-written opinion pieces. [www.nytimes.com/section/learning]

- The Ringer has a range of argumentative pieces on topics that rarely get meaningful arguments about them: sports, pop culture, and technology. [www.theringer.com]

- Teen Vogue has impressive writing on often high-interest topics for adolescents. [www.teenvogue.com]

- *The Week* is an online magazine with short weekly opinion pieces from a variety of political angles. [www.theweek.com]

What Is Metacognition, and Why Is It So Important?

In many ways, our brains are nearly limitless in their capacity. No hard cap exists on memories that can be created or skills that can be gained. But there are two functions of our brains that are incredibly limited: our attention and our working memory.

When it comes to our attention, as anyone who has ever tried to text and walk knows, we can only really pay attention to one thing at a time, and even when focusing on one thing, attention is a finite resource that runs low or out completely over time. In terms of working memory, or how much temporary information we can hold in our minds, there is some debate about the exact size, but it is relatively minute compared to other systems of memory (Doolittle, 2013).

Our limited attention and working memory have major implications for the ELA classroom, where so much of the work we do—reading critically, writing well, arguing persuasively—are massive cognitive jobs that require us to juggle a number of different tasks.

Serious readers and writers, consciously or unconsciously, generally understand this challenge, which is why nearly all engage in strategies that break these enormous tasks into manageable pieces. Readers often do this by underlining, highlighting, scrawling in the margins, planting sticky note after sticky note, and dog-earring pages until books can barely close. Writers often do it through revising robustly, joining writing groups, and assembling small arsenals of readers to help them see the gaps and problems that inevitably arise when one is composing something of depth.

Yet when one looks at classrooms, many students do not engage in these practices. They read without marking anything and write one draft and turn it in without another glance. It can be easy to get frustrated at these students because such approaches combined with our limitations place a hard cap on how deep one can dig into a piece of literature or how powerful of a piece one can write.

But as is so often the case in the classroom, students often don't use these tools because they don't understand why these things are of value. This is where teaching students metacognition comes in.

"Metacognition" is still a relatively new and buzzy term for many educators, but despite its relative newness, it is an idea with deep roots in academic research. Its common definition is "thinking about one's thinking," which is clever phrasing but hard at times to fully grasp. We prefer to look at metacognition as helping students to develop a user's manual for their own brains, and we do it by engaging in the following.

METACOGNITIVE STRATEGY #1: TALK BRAIN SCIENCE WITH STUDENTS

We've found that students love discussion of the brain as much as anyone. Some of the most interesting resources for seeding these conversations include the following:

- Dave likes to have his students read and discuss a *Guardian* interview with neuroscientist David Eagleman (Anthony, 2021). Among many fascinating insights, Dave's students always marvel at Eagleman's claim that during the reading of a single paragraph, our brains are changing. This helps them to understand just how plastic neuroplasticity really is. It also makes them sense the value of each act of reading they undertake.

- Matt Johnson shares the *Entrepreneur* magazine story " Why Multitasking Is a Myth That's Breaking Your Brain and Wasting Your Time" (Toren, 2017; QR in margin) with his students. It is a succinct, accessible rundown of key research findings about multitasking:

  - When we "multitask," we are actually switching between tasks and losing up to 40 percent of our time in the process.
  - Those who try to multitask make more mistakes and release more stress hormones than those who don't.
  - Many of the most successful people carefully plan when they will do commonly multitasked things like respond to emails or texts.

  This conversation generally leads naturally into a discussion of the tools we have to deal with our limited attention, like annotation or peer response.

Multitasking article to share with students

METACOGNITIVE STRATEGY #2: INCREASE REFLECTION

Reflection is something touted by teachers as an essential component of learning, but as Arthur L. Costa and Bena Kallick (2008) found, the actual use of reflection in schools is quite rare, with the next unit or paper generally getting far more attention than the learning that has passed. Costa and Kallick also argue that "such an orientation means that students (and teachers) find it easier to discard what has happened and to move on without taking stock of the seemingly isolated experiences of the past" (para. 5).

This tendency to let the past be past slows or limits the development of metacognition because one of the best ways to understand one's processes and skills is to review and dissect what one has already done. This is why coaches show athletes film from previous games and why therapists spend so much time asking about the past. When we look at what we've done before, the invisible workings of our minds can suddenly become visible, allowing us to proceed forward with a better understanding of who we are and how we work.

In our classes, reflection is a common practice, in part to do that steady work of building metacognition. Some of the main ways we do this include

- Letter writing

- Quarterly reflections

- Goal-setting that uses the results of previous units
- Quick reflections

> When we look at what we've done before, the invisible workings of our minds can suddenly become visible.

METACOGNITIVE STRATEGY #3: TEACH STUDENTS IN METACOGNITIVE PROCESSES

Project Zero
thinking routines

NSRF thinking protocols
(www.nsrfharmony.org)

A common and long-used metacognitive tool is to give students step-by-step routines that they can follow when doing some task to train them to approach it metacognitively. There are hundreds or even thousands of such metacognitive processes in professional development books, and they all follow the same basic three-step idea:

1. Identify a common problem.
2. Offer a potential solution.
3. Provide a tool that gives step-by-step guidance for how to overcome the problem.

A great many of these processes work well, with some of our favorites being the thinking routines from Harvard's Project Zero or the protocols from the National School Reform Faculty (view the QR codes in the margins for these protocols). Even still, anyone can create their own metacognitive processes by following the three listed steps.

Here is an example of what this looks like in practice:

Problem	Solution	Tool
Writing well means doing dozens of things well simultaneously, yet we can only notice one thing at a time and only hold a handful of things in our working memory.	We need to break our revision into different stages, devoting each stage to actively looking at different aspects of our writing.	Students create a writing checklist based on what they know about writing in general and their own writing that outlines the key steps they need to take during their revision.
Reading deeply means that one must do a lot well. You must first comprehend the text, then notice important details, then analyze those details, and finally express one's unique analysis clearly to someone else.	We need to train and guide students to break deep reading comprehension into simpler steps, so the overall task doesn't feel so daunting.	Teacher Marisa Thompson (n.d.) created the TQE (thoughts, questions, epiphanies) method for reading deeply. In TQE, students (1) write thoughts, questions, and epiphanies (TQE) as they read; (2) share those TQEs with a small group; (3) determine the strongest two for each category; and then (4) share those with the larger class, seeding a larger conversation. For more, visit Marisa's website, www.unlimitedteacher.com/tqe.

The goal of metacognition is to remove the blinders that we all wear when it comes to why, how, and what we do. This can be deeply effective and deeply empowering for students, many of whom may have felt previously shackled by struggles in drafting, close reading, or issues they didn't even know they had. Matt Johnson still remembers one student who came back a few years ago to show him the now-laminated writing review sheet she created in his class—a tool that she used for every one of the hundreds of papers she wrote as she pursued and achieved her BA in English literature (see Figure 4.1).

Figure 4.1 Example of a Targeted Checklist

A WRITING REVIEW: YOUR PERSONAL ESSAY

Please look over your paper and check the following:

☐ **Introduction**

Look at the introduction. Our mentor introductions used stories, scenes, and surprising facts to capture the reader's interest. How does yours compare to those? Do you use similar techniques or something else? Whatever you used, explain your approach and/or technique next to the first line. Then, once you've labeled your approach and/or technique, think about whether your intro feels as strong as the models. If it doesn't, try to improve it to make it stronger.

☐ **Linking Verbs**

Do a quick count of how many conjugations of *to be* you have on your first page. If you have more than five or six, look to eliminate some. If you have fewer than five or six, think about if there are any that need to be eliminated (remember, having some is fine; it's when you have too many that *to be* begins to be a problem).

☐ **Sentence Length and Parallel Structure**

Do a look for sentence length. Do you vary it? Is it used purposefully? Is there thoughtful parallel structure?

☐ **Characterization**

Look at how you explain who you are. Make a list in your notebook of the direct things you say about yourself and the indirect things you show. In looking at that list, is there any way to indirectly show some of the things you directly say? Generally speaking, showing is stronger than telling, so try to convert as many of the direct ones into indirect ones as you can.

☐ **Clichés**

Go on a cliché hunt. Highlight all potential college essay clichés (like, "I'm passionate about helping others, which is why I want to be a doctor") and replace as many as possible with personal stories and details (such as, "I have a cousin who spent the majority of his childhood in the hospital. I spent many long nights watching his doctors work . . .").

☐ **Everything Else**

After everything above, read it again (or more than once) for other key things. In doing this, think about other elements we've talked about and where you've struggled with previous papers.

INSTRUCTION

How Much Choice and Voice Should Students Have?

When planning instruction, one of the thorniest issues to grapple with is the amount of choice given to students. On the one hand, well-designed choice can bring the following benefits:

- It can be an important way to acknowledge students' individuality and agency.

- By having a place in class for students to plug in their own interests, choice can cultivate a sense in students that the work they are doing has value (see Chapter 2).

- Choice often leads students to high-interest topics and tasks—the types of topics and tasks that can lead to a dramatic increase in effort and engagement. We have likely all seen or even been those students who, when they have sufficient choice, can soar like a kite on a gusty day caught in an updraft.

But choice, while it can be a powerful force for good, is not a panacea. Some potential challenges with choice include the following:

- Too much choice can stand in the way of having a dialogic class. If every student is always reading their own choice of book, for example, you can't have in-depth discussions about characters or authorial decisions or themes. Instead, you end up needing to keep whole-class conversations superficial— for example, "In the book I'm reading, Author X did this, and it kind of sounds like what Student Y was talking about in her book by Author Z." This setup can rob students of the ability to learn from and work with each other— something that is crucial to how we run our classes.

- An imbalance of choice can pave the way for unhelpful or inequitable individualized outcomes. Students who came into the class with, say, a broader knowledge base can pick up a greater variety of books and gain a greater degree of new knowledge from those readings. Meanwhile, students with a narrower knowledge base might not be able to broaden their knowledge as much without the guidance of a teacher—guidance that can be split 30 or 35 times (depending on the number of students) in a mostly choice environment.

- Most teachers generally have required content to cover, skills to teach, and rubrics and standards to hit. This isn't necessarily a bad thing, as often the skills and content required are often incredibly important for living a vibrant, flourishing literary life.

This tension between choice, voice, community, and curriculum is not an easy one, and every year the three of us continue to experiment in the pursuit of finding that perfect balance. Still, we all believe the right approach is striving for balance.

Here are some of the specific tools, approaches, and lessons you can use to seek that balance:

- **Give lots of small and medium-sized writing assignments that build to larger, more open assignments.** The smaller and medium-sized assignments can ensure that students build specific skills and gain crucial knowledge—skills and knowledge that can then be leveraged in the pursuit of some larger, more organic topic.

- **Use lots of mentor texts that showcase different approaches** one could take to any given assignment. This will give students a sense for the myriad of possibilities that exist even in assignments that appear more closed.

- **Make space in class for independent reading.** We all include choice-based silent sustained reading (SSR) as a key in-class element each week. Matt Kay does it every Friday for 20 minutes, and students do quarterly independent creative projects that are to be inspired by their SSR texts. These projects can be anything from writing missing chapters to poetry collections to art projects (with writing components); view the QR in the margin for an example of a project Matt Kay's student teacher, Mr. Davis, assigned in 2021. Matt Johnson does choice reading twice a week for 25 minutes, with weekly book group discussions where students share what they've been reading with peers and Matt.

Example SSR project

- **Allow for choice within how students can approach many papers/projects.** Many of our papers and projects have no prompt at all. Instead, we ask students to create papers/projects of their own design based on content from class. If you take this approach, we highly recommend an idea that Troy Hicks and Andy Schoenborn describe in *Creating Confident Writers* (2020), where they have students submit proposals for more open-ended assignments so that they can keep the projects organized and to act as an early warning about which students are struggling with the choice or going down paths that might not meet the criteria. Figure 4.2 shows a proposal form Matt Johnson uses in his current ELA classes.

- **Create book clubs.** At least once a year, Matt Kay has students pick a text from a group of five or six options. Most recently, the ninth graders picked memoirs, and the 10th graders picked dystopian novels. He groups the students who pick the same book, then works the unit like a book club. While the writing remains individual, each group leads a short lesson for their classmates on the ways that the author of their book engages readers.

- **Frame whole-class work around themes, questions, and assessments that allow for space.** When Matt Johnson's ninth graders read Maya Angelou's (1969) *I Know Why the Caged Bird Sings* together, they keep revisiting a central question: What can we learn from this personal story about overcoming adversity with vibrancy and grace? When it comes time for the final paper/project, students use everything we've discussed as the starting point to pursue this question in any way they want. (Remember how we told you in Chapter 1 that we ask students to keep a notebook of their classmates' comments during discussion? That comes in handy here!)

In the end, there probably is no perfect ratio of choice to guaranteed curriculum. At times, the balance of choice and voice and the needs of curriculum might shift one way or another, depending on the needs of the class, the age of the students, the time of year, and a thousand other factors. Still, given the potential power and pitfalls, offering choice and voice should be one of the biggest considerations in instructional planning, right alongside scope and standards when we are planning out our lessons, unit, and year.

Figure 4.2 Example Proposal for a Narrative Paper From Matt J.'s Classes

Storytelling Paper Proposal

Please fill out the following form with your proposal for your paper

What is your name?

Short answer text

What type of story will you be writing?

Long answer text

What are the basic details of the story? Take a couple sentences to sketch it out. Why did you choose that particular story?

Long answer text

What is one writing goal you have for yourself on this paper? How will I know if you have successfully reached your goal? What will success for your goals look like?

Long answer text

What Are the Essentials of an Impactful Reading/Writing Conference?

Conferences are the beating heart of the reading/writing workshop model of teaching, and they are a common suggestion from a great many master educators for some very good reasons:

- Conferences allow for an opportunity to discover gaps or holes in understanding and build bridges across those gulfs. Students misunderstanding or misinterpreting teacher feedback, classroom content, and expectations can sometimes be the norm, as opposed to the exception (Chanock, 2000), and conferences can help overcome that challenge.

- Conferences allow teachers to personalize instruction, which is particularly important for helping those who have fraught relationships with reading and writing (The Reading & Writing Project, n.d.).

- Conferences invite students in as active partners, not passive vessels waiting to be filled with information.

- As one of the main one-to-one points of contact between students and teachers, conferences can help to build strong relationships between students and teachers. In fact, in many classes the time spent individually with students in conferences is more than all other time spent individually with them combined. This makes conferences a critical place for building and maintaining positive relationships with students.

For these reasons and more, conferences have widespread usage in elementary classrooms, but conferencing is far more rare in middle and high school classrooms, likely because the average secondary teacher has both more content to deliver and far less time with students.

 Conferences are the beating heart of the reading/ writing workshop model of teaching.

Given their many advantages, we all engage in conferences with our students, but we also are careful about how we structure them, using the following approaches to maximize their impact while minimizing the time they require:

- **Students do the prep work for the conference.** Dr. Deanna Mascle of Morehead State University suggests having the students do the work setting the agenda and generally preparing for the needs of the conference in advance (Mascle, 2016). This inversion of the classic conference structure where teachers speak first and students respond allows the conferences to do more in less time because the discussion skips the preamble and starts with the personalized needs of the students. The prep work also adds an extra layer of student reflection and metacognition upon both their writing and the teacher's feedback.

- **Teachers go to the students.** Having students make the trek to the teacher's desk can subtly reinforce the dynamic that conferences exist mainly for teachers to talk and students to listen. Try instead either having conferences at student desks or hosting conferences in a neutral place, as that small physical shift can act as a potent signal that this conversation is about working together as partners.

- **Teachers record key points of the conference.** Holding the content of 150 or 160 conferences in one's mind is not possible for most people, especially as the days and weeks go by. These limits of memory can also limit meaningful follow-ups after conferences and lead to subsequent conferences that rehash the same territory in ways that are not ideal. When teachers take short notes concerning the conference, though, they can much more effectively hold onto the valuable content of those conversations, which can be useful for everything from improving conferences the next time to providing more personalized feedback.

- **Keep the conference focused.** In the same way that, when we try to respond to everything in a paper, we can respond to nothing (at least not in a way that leads to lasting learning), the same can be true for conferences. Trying to cover too much in a conference often means a lot of time gets spent on not nearly enough lasting gain. This is why during a conference we behave in the same way we do when providing feedback: We focus on a few things and go deep.

- **Do more reading and writing in class.** The classic ELA class structure is for reading and writing to happen at home while class time is populated with teacher lectures, group work, and whole-class discussions. While students can certainly learn a great deal from teachers and their classmates, the most important factor when it comes to learning to read and write is *how much students read and write*. To outsource all or most of that to home is a big part of the reason why students can get away with going years without actually reading or writing much of anything. This is why we strive to have a large percentage of our class time (roughly 30–50 percent, depending on the class) devoted to students actively reading and writing. An additional benefit of doing this is that it makes conferencing, even in the biggest classes, a relative breeze because each week there are dozens or even hundreds of minutes available to talk reading and writing with students.

How Can I Do Direct Instruction Well? (What Should Be Done With the Lecture?)

"Lecture" is often a bad word in middle and high school ELA education circles, but we need to unpack it a bit to understand why. The common way of talking about lecture conjures the picture of a sleeping classroom of students with a self-entertaining teacher at the front of the class, spouting endlessly about the Romantics or iambic pentameter or thesis statements. This caricature is, pretty obviously, a terrible way to teach.

Historically, it's also been way too common, and that's led to the catchy sayings that effective secondary ELA teachers should only be "guides on the side" rather than "sages on stages."

So doesn't that settle it then? No lecture—ever?

Not quite. Remember, the objective of our classrooms is to help our students become better thinkers, readers, writers, speakers, listeners, and people. We're secondary ELA educators, not pedagogical robots. And so, for a given lesson segment, we may want to use some direct instruction—some "sage on the stage" in miniature, if you will.

But for direct instruction to be effective, here are a few rules of thumb:

- **People can only hold so much in their minds at a time.** Focus your direct instruction on one or two clear objectives. Do not ramble; do not overload. If you do, you'll start seeing the glazed-over expressions that come with information overwhelm.

- **Students remember what they actively think about.** This means you want to be sure to pepper direct instruction with opportunities for students—all students, not just those with hands raised—to process, discuss, write, ask questions, or argue.

- **Never speak uninterrupted for more minutes than the grade level of your students.** For example, for ninth graders, direct instruction shouldn't go unbroken beyond nine minutes—but that doesn't mean *aim* for nine minutes! Class time is precious, and direct instruction almost always makes you the hardest thinker in the room. So aim to make it as efficient as possible, which leaves more time for things like discussion, conferring, reading, or writing.

What Is Project-Based Learning (PBL), and How Does It Fit With a Reading and Writing Classroom?

Project-based learning centers learning around the thoughtful completion of an artifact of learning. When explaining the impact of this form of teaching on teachers' day-to-day practice, Matt Kay's principal at Science Leadership Academy, Chris Lehmann, often asks people to imagine two pyramids that look like the food pyramid that folks the authors' age might remember from the 1990s. The first pyramid is meant to represent a "traditional" classroom (see Figure 4.3a). At the bottom, where the 6 to 11 servings of carbs used to go, he put tests and quizzes. This represents the typically heavy grading weight of tests and the enormous energy spent preparing kids for them. The top, where we still find fats and sugars, is where the "traditional" classroom places projects. This represents the way that projects are often used just to sweeten up the class experience (like sugar). In the second pyramid (see Figure 4.3b), meant to represent a project-based classroom, Lehmann flips it. He recommends many "servings" of projects, which should be the core of our diet. Tests and quizzes, at the top with the "junk food," are to be used sparingly (maybe to check whether kids did their reading) or not used at all.

Figure 4.3a and 4.3b Traditional vs. PBL "Servings"

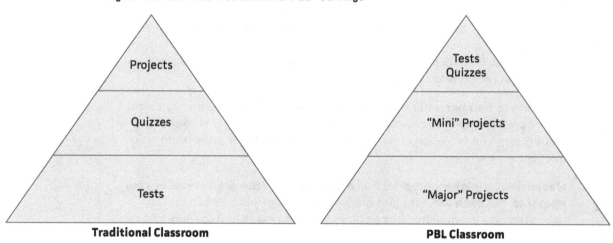

This PBL pyramid is a good way to check how project-based our ELA classroom is at any given moment. For instance, measure your instruction against these questions, *if you're trying to incorporate a more project-based instructional style*:

- Which assessments weigh more in our gradebooks?

- When discussing any given text, are there more factual, reading-comprehension prompts (as if to prepare students for tests) or more higher-order prompts (to prepare them for both analytical and creative writing projects, as well as various forms of presentations)?

- When practicing writing, how many minutes are spent preparing students for the kind of writing they are likely to see on tests (short answer, etc.) versus how much time is spent teaching students skills they'll need for longer-form writing projects?

- When students are trying to just make it to the finish line, and we can't realistically do both, which of the two forms of instruction and learning do we focus on—traditional or PBL?

- Which do we more often ask students to commit their emotional energy to? To be proudest of?

Notes

INSTRUCTION

How Do We Help Our Students Remember Things?

A common understanding of our brains is that they are built for remembering things. This understanding explains the design of many of the classic instructional methods like the aforementioned lecture, the textbook, or the flashcard. These methods share the common trait that they are far more focused on giving information than they are interested in helping students to hold onto that information.

The problem with overrelying on these methods is that students are not just empty pitchers waiting to be filled with information. Instead, students (and the rest of us) are, according to neurobiologists Blake Richards and Paul Frankland, in many ways designed more for forgetting than for remembering. Richards and Frankland (2017) argue that considering how many neural connections exist in our heads, we could remember dramatically more than we do. But in a world that is noisy, always changing, and full of nuance, the ability to forget most of what we see and hear is essential when it comes to fulfilling the purpose of memory: using information from the past to better navigate the future.

So, the question then becomes, if our brains are more suited for forgetting than remembering, what can be done to ensure that the important content from our classes isn't among the information pruned when our students' brains do their regular scrubbing? Here are a few possible solutions:

USE RETRIEVAL/SPACING/INTERLEAVING

In *Powerful Teaching*, Pooja Agarwal and Patrice Bain examine three tools that, along with feedback, help turn student predispositions to forget into predispositions to remember (2019, pp. 4–5):

- **Retrieval** is the act of trying to find or retrieve information from one's mind. Doing this prompts the brain to flag the information as important since you are trying to pull it up and use it. In response to this flag, the brain makes it more accessible, almost like a thumbnail added to a desktop.

- **Spacing** is where, by spreading out when one retrieves and uses information, it once again tells the brain that this isn't just information needed for one isolated moment; it is something important enough that you continue to come back to it, and thus it needs to be preserved and protected.

- **Interleaving** is the idea that when information is used in different ways— for example, using research skills in a research paper *and* also crafting a rebuttal during a class debate or checking the veracity of an article that one is critiquing—it will also be seen by the brain as being potentially more relevant and worthy of storage and potentially rapid access.

The root of all three tools is the same problem: Our brains will look to forget things only encountered once because if we never think of them again they likely aren't relevant to our long-term survival. Within that problem is offered a simple antidote for our classes: To give students' brains a better chance at memory, we simply need to make sure that they encounter all critical information multiple times on multiple days and ideally use it in multiple ways.

TIME = IMPORTANCE

In introductory film classes and screenwriting books, the mantra that *Time = Importance* is often repeated. When writing or directing a half-hour show or two-hour film, every single second is essential real estate. Moments that don't actively move the plot along or persuade us to fall in love (or hate) with a character take the space of some other moment that could. Add up enough lost opportunities, and that is often what separates a perennial classic from something seasonal that wilts not long after it blooms.

The same advice could easily be given in introductory teaching courses. While 180 days of school may look like a lot, any seasoned teacher knows that it is not nearly enough to fit it all in once things get rolling. This is why careful planning is necessary.

- **Carefully sketch out each semester in advance.** The three of us have had years where we were just a day or an hour ahead, which is why we know that finding an afternoon before the school year begins to clearly lay out what we hope to achieve and how we will get there can save five times those hours once the school year begins.

- **Commit to assessment dates before school begins, especially with same-course colleagues.** A critical part of semester sketching is determining when we'll give unit assessments or collect summative writing assignments. This helps avoid wasting what seems like infinite time at the start of a semester only to find ourselves in dire straits as the semester closes and we're cramming in one last unit. By deciding before the course starts when we'll give unit assessments or collect unit papers, we bind ourselves to constraints that help us monitor and adapt how we're using our time.

- **Sometimes, you have to kill your darlings.** When we love a text or prompt or activity, we often don't notice how much space it takes and whether that space is worth the results we get. Carefully looking at everything—and especially our favorite lessons/stories/novels/projects—from the perspective of the time cost relative to student benefit is often a good idea, and if something isn't worth the time invested, we should probably get rid of it.

USE UNDERSTANDING BY DESIGN (UBD) TO KEEP EVERYTHING CLEAR

McTighe's UbD template online

Grant Wiggins and Jay McTighe's *Understanding by Design* (2005) advises us to always plan our units with the end in mind. This classic backward planning approach can help us to ensure that we give proper time and repetition to the collection of skills and thought processes that matter in each unit. Here are a few pro tips for more efficient and useful UbD planning:

- McTighe offers a template for us to use for unit planning, and many more can be found online. Remember that we can add whatever "extra" boxes that we might need (view the QR in the margin to get to McTighe's template site).

  For instance, Matt Kay adds boxes for these things:
  - **Supplementary readings.** Placing hyperlinks of any online readings or videos directly in the UbD unit plan as soon you find them ensures that you aren't caught right before a class trying to find an essential resource.
  - **Our school's core values and how the unit will engage them.** The clear written engagement of the school's core values (or mission statement or anything like that) will make it that much easier to justify curricular choices that may be unpopular.
  - **General things to watch out for.** A box for general things—which Matt Kay calls "Tips/Tools"—is where he reminds himself of likely minefields in conversation, connections that excited students, or possible supplementary games and activities. Basically, it's a series of notes that he writes himself for next year so that he makes his worst teaching mistakes *only* once and calls his best audibles *more than* once!

- Take advantage of the concise nature of UbD unit plans (two or three pages at max!) versus an endless stack of daily lesson plans. The snapshot that they provide presents not only a wonderful opportunity for interdisciplinary planning with colleagues but also a way to get kids involved in the planning for future units.

Notes

How Can Mentor Texts Be Used to Accelerate Writing Skills?

When we read great writing with young writers, the goal is respect, not awe. While fandom is OK, we don't want our students to worship the Shakespeares, Morrisons, Wrights, and Acevedos as if their writing talents were given at birth and are therefore unattainable. After reading something spectacular, we want students to think, "How did they do that?" Then, after learning how, we want them to say, "Let me try." Then finally, after the first few successes, "Look! I did that!"

The secret to going from "How did they do that?" to "Look! I did that" is the regular use of mentor texts, or texts chosen to offer examples, guidance, and possibilities. In our classes, we use mentor texts constantly, but most tend to fall into one of three categories.

STAND-ALONE ACTIVITIES THAT PRACTICE THE SKILLS FOUND IN MENTOR TEXTS

- **Juicy Sentences**. Inspired by ELA teacher Emma Tsai (2019), Matt Kay asks students to first collect "juicy" sentences in the texts that they read together and then use versions of two or three of them in the unit's final creative project. To make this work, first point out different types of sentences in a piece of writing, such as an article or passage from a class novel, that stand out to you as particularly effective. For instance, call attention to a "short, punchy sentence" ("All he wanted was that view") and one with "a strong verb" ("All cancers have the power to ravage a body, but each assails in distinctive ways"). Then, ask students to read and pick sentences that they—for whatever reason—deem well written. Students then must replicate *their own versions* of the sentences in their own creative writing. They can do this by "adding an impactful introductory sentence, incorporating introductory clauses, varying sentence length, diversifying verb choice or anything else" (Tsai, 2019, p. x). The final product looks like this:

  - **Example**: "But not long afterward, I began to hate her, due not to the foolishness of her idea but because of her absurd and unyielding confidence in it."
  - **Student**: But not long afterward, I was filled with regret, not because I fully understood her words, but because I knew in my gut they were right.

- **Craft Lessons**. Matt Johnson found that a large part of what made so many of his students dislike writing was that they simply didn't know how it worked. They had no idea what gave a sentence "flow" or how to add emphasis to a moment that really mattered because nobody had ever told them. Now, as a way of building both skills and confidence, Matt does weekly craft lessons aimed at expanding the students' writing toolboxes and making clearer to them how writing can work. (The online companion, resources.corwin.com/answersELA, hosts some downloadable examples of craft lessons.)

DOMESTICATED AND WILD MENTOR TEXTS

Students regularly get asked to write an essay or compose a research paper without ever seeing a single example of one, which makes the already difficult task of composing something meaningful unnecessarily harder. In our classes, we look at two distinctly different types of mentor text before composing anything:

- **Domesticated Mentor Texts.** These are texts composed by previous students. When we say domesticated, we don't mean that they are all calm or cookie-cutter. Instead, we mean that these are examples whose genesis happened within the walls of a classroom. We strive to use a wide range of examples, and just like some domesticated cats or dogs can act somewhat undomesticated, so can some of our examples.

- **Wild Mentor Texts.** Wild mentor texts are ones that arose outside the classroom. These are texts created for purposes other than getting a grade or fulfilling the criteria of an assignment. Many are from professional writers, but we also strive to use plenty from adolescents and those whose paychecks don't come for writing. It is also worth noting that they aren't all exactly "wild" in their approach, with their tone, style, and approach running a wide gamut.

Using the UbD approach, introduce these texts early and often during units so that, when it comes time for things like drafting, peer review, and self-assessments, the students already have lots of examples to help them frame their approaches.

INFORMAL MENTOR TEXTS

When we read something in class that makes students (or in some awkward moments, just us) exclaim "Ooooh," we make a show of pointing out and explaining what, specifically, the author did to draw this kind of response. These organic mentor moments are quick, but potentially because of the surprise factor, they can often be the moments that stick with students and shift their writing the most.

We also look for moments to work in mentor texts from the opposite angle. When you see a student do something really cool, try pulling them aside and show them a published author that does the same stuff. This can be a powerful identity-building moment.

Notes

What Role Can Emotions (Surprise, Uncertainty, Joy, Anger) Play in Instruction?

Matt Johnson recalls guidance from a veteran in his first year that as a new teacher he "should not smile before Thanksgiving." This kind of guidance, while once commonplace, has thankfully largely gone by the wayside, yet its residue remains. Teachers often don't think about the role of emotion—either theirs or the emotions of their students—when planning lessons and units. It's too bad because emotion, when strategically used, can be a powerful tool and ally. And, be warned, emotion when it goes wrong can stop learning in an instant. With that in mind, here are some things that are worth thinking about when it comes to using emotions in the class.

A note, too, before reading on: Please read this section through the lens of community building described in Chapter 2. We do not want to let decisions about the emotional life of our curriculum threaten the work that we do to build a strong community of readers and writers.

JOY

In her book *Teaching for Joy and Justice*, Linda Christensen writes the following of teaching for and with joy: "It's what our students need. But it's also what we need" (2009, p. 11). Her acknowledgment that a class of joy can sustain and elevate both the students and the teacher is an important one because so often joy is framed as a peripheral emotion when it comes to teaching—one that is nice if it happens but is by no means essential. Christensen's framing of joy as central consideration if we want our classes to be their best matches what we've seen in our own classes. We now purposefully cultivate joy in a number of ways, with the following being some of the most effective.

SWEAT THE SMALL STUFF

- Debate and argumentation in classes don't have to be confined to just the text you're reading. As a way of building community (and one that is surprisingly effective), we will regularly debate the silly stuff too. Do pineapples belong on a pizza? What is the ultimate walk-up song? Whose cheesesteaks are the best?

- Sometimes, we misinterpret students' passion during a conversation as immaturity or disrespect. This one is short: Let them get excited!

LOOK FOR AND REVEL IN THE POETRY

In *We Got This*, Cornelius Minor explains how he tries to meet all kids with the question of "Where is the poetry in this young person?" (2018, p. 13). This is sound advice, and it is often echoed in different words (like having an asset-based approach instead of a deficit-based one), but we've found this notion of looking for poetry to be useful in remembering to take joy in the strengths, skills, and growth students display on a regular basis.

What Role Can Emotions (Surprise, Uncertainty, Joy, Anger) Play in Instruction?

113

WRITE ON JOYFUL PROMPTS

A great way to infuse joy into the ELA classroom is to regularly use writing prompts that inspire joy. The exact right joyful prompt is going to depend on the combination of the class, teacher, and students, but the key is to be on the lookout for joyful prompts. Here is an example of this approach that involves two of us: In the spring of 2021, Matt Kay found a massive tray of untouched and delicious-looking macaroni and cheese in the park on his way to school. He tweeted about it, and Matt Johnson shared the tweet with his students and then asked them to write an origin story about the mac-and-cheese that was filled with strong examples of the lesson for the day (imagery). The results had the whole class in stitches, as the surprising and often shocking origins of the park mac-and-cheese were revealed, and the imagery was the best Matt J. had ever seen from any class.

SURPRISE

Surprise can be remarkably effective at shifting the way students views themselves or the world around them. In his book *The Power of Surprise: How Your Brain Secretly Changes Your Beliefs*, Michael Rousell (2021) explains how surprise is a psychological signal to the brain that something about how we see the world is wrong. This signal then opens our brains to recognize change in a way that they don't normally because if something is wrong with how we see the world, then we need to shift something about our perception of the world.

Rousell explains that, because of the power that surprise has, in his classes he is always on the lookout for ways that he can use it to help his students. For example, he points out that learning in ELA is often slow and fairly invisible to the students themselves, so when he is working on writing or reading he will be on the lookout for moments when students express frustration about not growing (or not growing as quickly as they like), maybe by saying something like "I move so slowly." Then, he does the following: "Just as [the students] feel down [for being slow], I'd laugh or give some expression they don't expect. Something like 'Ha! Your slow, careful work makes you learn it better.' If the comment surprises them, they get a hit of phasic dopamine. That's a neurological error signal that says learn instantly" (M. Rousell, personal communication, November 27, 2021). And the hope is that the positive moment of surprise created here will help the student to suddenly see their slowness as an asset—as a marker of doing the work deeply and well—as opposed to a sign that they are not a very strong student.

DISCOMFORT

More attention has been paid recently to the importance of giving students a more proper orientation before both reading emotionally challenging texts and having emotionally challenging classroom conversations. This includes, but is not limited to, the practice of giving "trigger warnings." If a text contains a scene that depicts abuse, sexual harassment or assault, or trauma, many counsel teachers to give students a heads-up so that they might either emotionally prepare themselves or step out of class.

This practice, like so many in this era, has become deeply—and needlessly—politicized. Learning is, by definition, uncomfortable. Students, like all of us, generally think they know more than they actually do, and as with surprise, learning new information destabilizes them for a while until they find balance. Then, the cycle repeats. Although some discomfort is necessary, there is a clear line where discomfort impedes learning and hurts students instead of being a natural part of learning that will ultimately uplift them. Students should always feel safe. While discomfort is a natural part of the learning process, feeling unsafe never, under any circumstances, should be. Here are some ways that we ensure that our students feel safe:

Keep in Mind

Be wary of activities and lessons that expect shock to do most of the teaching (privilege walks, role playing, etc.). Without strong pedagogical choices surrounding it, this form of engagement might not just be ineffective, it might also be traumatizing to our students.

- **Teach students their reader's rights.** Before reading potentially difficult texts, we have an open discussion about their rights as readers. We approach these conversations differently in our different classrooms, but they all revolve around the same central idea: If a book ever makes you feel unsafe, we encourage you to close it and come talk to us. No student in our classes will ever lose points because they stopped reading a book that crossed that safety line for them.

- **Find a balance between mindful orientation and letting students feel things authentically.** Sometimes, the earnest spirit behind "trigger warnings" leads us to unnecessarily spoil the books that we teach. We start off teaching a book by highlighting all the depressing parts, focusing on the wrong real-world debates about it, or even by overdoing the literary lens focus ("We're going to look at this play through the feminist or new historicist lens!") instead of letting kids come to these lenses organically. While we should be thoughtful about not traumatizing or retraumatizing students by withholding crucial information, we also don't want to rob books of the chance to make kids feel things.

- **Understand all the cultural dynamics at play during emotionally intense class discussions.** For instance, Matt Kay uses a YouTube video in one of his professional development sessions where a teacher hosts a classroom debate on Colin Kaepernick's kneeling protest. The teacher in the video reminds his students that "the big thing is respect" and that "if it gets vulgar, I will have to ask you to step out." This teacher is essentially asking for "classiness" or "professionalism"—common asks for many teachers before intense discussions. This "classy/professional" ruleset, though, is tested a few minutes later when a student says, "If [Kaepernick] doesn't like it here, he can just leave." This isn't vulgar on the surface, but consider this statement from the perspective of an immigrant student. For that student, there might not be a big difference between a calm "If you don't like it, you can leave" and a shouted "If you don't like it, you can f_____ leave!" Furthermore, if the kid with an immigrant experience uses profanity in his response to this clear trolling, does he deserve to be kicked from class while the instigator stays? This example begs the question, what is "classy," "professional," "vulgar," or "respectful"? What do these words mean in our class discussions, and why? These important definitions and distinctions need to be made clear to students up front and repeated often.

INSTRUCTION

chapter FIVE

HOW CAN I KEEP DOING THIS FOR MY WHOLE CAREER?

In drafting this chapter, we quickly realized it could be its own book—and some of the early reviewers of this book rightly said as much. But the three of us strongly felt that it still belonged in *this* book too. Here's why:

☐ At the time that we're writing this in the fall of 2021, the United States is watching an unsustainably large number of teachers leaving the profession for early retirement or new careers. We authors still believe that teaching is the best job in the world, but we get it when we hear yet another colleague say, "I can't keep doing this." On default settings, the secondary ELA teacher's job isn't sustainable.

☐ We have found in our own careers that there are ways around the unsustainable default conditions of teaching—that, despite many broken systems and unjust arrangements, it's still possible to do a good job teaching and have a life. But to do that requires intention, decision-making, and strategy.

To help with that, we've provided the following questions and responses. But before we begin, it's important to note that matters of teacher longevity are even more personal and idiosyncratic than matters of classroom practice. All teachers have their own living conditions, relational circumstances, life pressures, capacities, and needs. We've included in the following pages what's worked to keep *us* in the game. We hope they help you too.

> On default settings, the secondary ELA teacher's job isn't sustainable.

Here are the questions we tackle in this final chapter:

- [ ] **How do we know which of the "smaller" classroom management issues are worth engaging?**
- [ ] **How can colleagues be your squad instead of the crabs in your barrel?**
- [ ] **How can the right extracurriculars give energy instead of taking it?**
- [ ] **How can I manage the unspoken expectations placed on teachers?**
- [ ] **As a teacher, when (and how) should I say no?**
- [ ] **How can I stay a writer while teaching writing? How about a reader while teaching reading?**
- [ ] **How can professional learning and professional communities keep you excited about teaching—and help you work faster and better?**
- [ ] **I'm bringing home work on nights and weekends, and it's driving me/my friends/my partner crazy. What can I do?**
- [ ] **How can I avoid burnout?**
- [ ] **What's the best way to get better as a teacher?**

How Do We Know Which of the "Smaller" Classroom Management Issues Are Worth Engaging?

Matt Kay hates when students have their backpacks on their desks (backpacks on desks block his view of students' hands). However, he doesn't mind when students are *occasionally* 15 seconds late to class because they were finishing up a hallway conversation with a friend (if certain kids are in a better mood to start off class, it makes *everyone's* life easier). He never lets students raise a hand when a classmate is talking. However, he doesn't mind some raised voices when a debate gets hot.

If we want to make a career of teaching in the classroom, we've got to understand the difference between "I care deeply about this!" and "I feel like I *should* care deeply about this!" We have a finite amount of capital to spend "checking" students for classroom faux pas; the more we waste on the latter, the less we have for the former. It stinks to notice a near-consensus among students that we are a "mean" teacher because we've feigned too much anger enforcing *someone else's* idea of what a good classroom looks like. This leads us down the path of harming our credibility *and* our students' sense of belonging.

To determine what's most important to reinforce in your class—and what you can let go of—we recommend these important reflections:

- What student behaviors really get under your skin? Why?

- What student behaviors *should* get under your skin, but you can't really muster the energy to care? Why don't you care?

- In both, how much capital are you willing to spend to "manage" this issue? Is this the best use of this capital?

After this reflection, your own personal "rules" or "pet peeves" might now become a section of your classes' community agreements (see Chapter 2). It is all right to be honest about them. Being open and clear about how and why we will manage the class can help to build credibility and community—if our justification is well thought out. It also can act as a natural starting point for seeking student contributions concerning the pet peeves they have and the rules they'd like to see as a part of the class as well.

Equity and Access

Our own pet peeves must be analyzed through the lens of equity and access. What cultures might be privileged by our more personal rules? Do some of our personal rules take into account different learning styles and physical abilities? Are we recognizing that we are not our students' first teacher, and they might have learned (and gotten good at) different acceptable behavior before they got to us?

How Can Colleagues Be Your Squad Instead of the Crabs in Your Barrel?

We won't be the first veteran teachers to advise new teachers to avoid colleagues that spread negative energy. This won't be the only book that tells you to avoid that toxic corner of the staff lounge or the gossipy back row of the staff meeting. We certainly won't be the only teachers who will advise you to give the jaded few among us a wide berth, especially those who disparage the students we serve. It's important to protect whatever positive energy you bring to your work and to the kids in your classroom.

You have to find your squad—the thought partners that you can kick unit plan ideas around with, the group that will build you back up after tough lessons fail and shout you out when you nail it.

These suggestions seem pretty straightforward and maybe a bit self-evident, but it is worth noting that teachers finding true squads is, in our experience, rare, while teachers getting stuck in a barrel of crabs trying to pull them down is not. So it is worth digging a bit deeper and thinking about how we can make sure that we are managing colleague relationships the right way:

- **When it comes to distancing yourself from colleagues who seem to revel in negativity, try doing it without being preachy**—especially as a teacher who is new to the environment who may not understand the complexity of your colleagues' frustrations. Do you have enough personal history with your school's administration to disprove your colleagues' instinctive lack of trust? Have you sat in this school's professional development meetings long enough to realize the same patterns that make colleagues roll their eyes? Have you taught long enough, in this school or at all, to have been overwhelmed by the specific challenges that your students present? If the answer is no, then resist the urge to sermonize. This doesn't mean, of course, that you join any chorus of negativity. It means that you humble yourself enough to understand that teachers, including yourself, will have human responses to frustration that require grace. Otherwise, you risk being pulled into a different type of negativity: one that can be as toxic as the negativity you are criticizing.

- **When colleagues have the energy to do something cool, help them out!** If you have a prep, step in as a guest judge for that history colleague's mock trial. Watch your engineering colleague's egg-drop contest. Taste-test the kids' final projects in your colleague's culinary arts unit. The loss of a prep is likely often going to feel like a major deal—and indeed that must be factored in (see discussion about unspoken expectations in Chapter 5)—but the energy and camaraderie that can come from helping with something cool is often worth it!

- **Understand that colleagues may not be able to help you in the same way.** Naturally, if you help colleagues out, you might eventually ask for their help too. It's important, however, to not be too upset if, at that moment, they decline because they are busy. We all need time to grade papers, make midday adjustments to lesson plans, or simply to chill out for an entire prep period and watch YouTube videos. Make sure that, in trying to make these connections, you understand this. Still, it's worth it to make the effort.

- **Connect around a shared passion.** The best squads we've seen have congealed around shared passions that exist inside or outside the school. Seek those who also want to work on making the school more equitable, explore ways to offer more cross-curricular instruction, or simply love "button poetry." Having that nucleus of a shared passion can help the squad to stay more focused on positive things and fight off the tempting descent into gossip and complaints.

- **Accept and offer social invitations.** We know you are tired, but say yes to that happy-hour invitation every once in a while, especially when it comes from colleagues who have positive energy. More importantly, make offers on your own.

How Do I Ensure My Administration Has My Back—and What Do I Do When I Feel Like They Don't?

Of all your school colleague relationships, those with administrators can be some of the most difficult because of the uneven power dynamic; however, all three of us can think of at least one principal whom we would consider to be an essential and positive part of our journeys. There are also principals in our history who were less than ideal and with whom our relationships weren't always perfect. We've found, though, that, whatever the state of the relationship between you and your principal, the ways to build, improve, or positively maintain it are strikingly similar to the suggestions in this section. They include the following:

- **Accept invitations and offer your own.** That means going to that optional free lunch instead of responding to a few extra papers or invite the principal to your room when the students are giving a really cool presentation.
- **Look for moments to connect with an administrator over a shared goal or interest.** As with your colleagues, working together on something that both parties are interested in is one of the best ways to build a strong foundation of mutual respect. While we don't recommend jumping at every new venture or constantly floating a new committee, be on the lookout for areas of shared interest.
- **Try to stay positive.** Even if there is plenty worth criticizing about an administrator, the incessant negative administrator talk so often present in the teacher's lounge or the back row of the staff meeting can be toxic for your well-being and the relationship with your administrator. It is worth seeing the positives and looking for ways to offer support so that you can work with that person for the betterment of your students.

How Can the Right Extracurriculars Give Energy Instead of Taking It?

The first few years in the classroom redefine our relationship to the word "busy." There's the time spent reading and rereading class texts. There's the hunt for (and curation of) useful supplementary sources. There's the unit and lesson planning, the school-assigned duties and meetings, and *all* the feedback and assessment required. With all of this (and so much more), the thought of making time for extracurricular activities is enough to give many new teachers heart palpitations. This is understandable, yet there are many ways that getting involved in extracurricular activities can *give* new ELA teachers energy, not sap it away. Here is what has worked for us:

- **Use extracurricular activities to get to know students better.** When coaching a sport or sponsoring a club, make sure that you take the time to learn students' histories and passions. This information will not just come in handy if you teach those students, but it will also help you get to know students who share the same interests.

- **Use extracurricular activities to help students get to know *you* better.** So many of the coaches in Matt Kay's slam poetry league have noticed a big difference in their in-school reputation after starting their school's slam team. Suddenly, they are "the poetry lady" or "that writer dude." Suddenly, previously unknown students show up to their classrooms to ask if they can read something they are working on. Of course, we should let kids get to know us in class, but it's so much easier to be our fullest nerd/sports fan/theater geek selves when working with kids outside of class. These reputations help us build student relationships that otherwise may not have blossomed.

- **Help colleagues with their clubs.** As the authors know from experience, it can be *hard* to run a club. We are always looking for more colleagues and adult volunteers to help. If we don't want to *direct* a play, maybe we can help with lighting, coach up the actors, help recruit kids, or pick up the snacks. We don't have to be in charge to get the benefits. Also, the more we help, the less time we might find ourselves hunting for help.

- **Let the extracurricular work supplement the "on-the-clock" curriculum.** As ELA teachers, we can certainly use resources originally meant for extracurricular activities in our classrooms. Matt Kay has used imagination builders from the improv club to practice public speaking during a rhetoric unit. He's used sample poems from slam poetry practice in a memoir unit. Dave Stuart has used things he's learned about in some of the clubs he's sponsored (e.g., Japanese Culture Club) as fodder for moments of genuine connection with students.

How Can the Right Extracurriculars Give Energy Instead of Taking It?

121

How Can I Manage the Unspoken Expectations Placed on Teachers?

In her book *Fewer Things, Better*, Angela Watson (2019) recounts the history of public education in America:

> In the early days of what's now evolved into our public school system in the United States, women teachers were required to be single and childless. They didn't juggle work/life balance because the expectation was that they wouldn't have much of a personal life apart from teaching. The profession was seen by many as a calling which one should whole-heartedly devote one's life to (much like a nun). . . . It was seen by many as unskilled labor which focused on imparting morality rather than intellectual skills or academics. As you would expect for a profession that was viewed this way, paltry wages were the norm. (pp. 32–33)

Watson goes on to name the unspoken expectations placed on teachers: Teachers should work through lunches and breaks, nights and weekends; accept the pay given to them while paying for materials themselves; and continually and unquestioningly add more to their plates to make up for any gaps that arise due to disinvestment from the school/district/state.

We can't recall ever being told these expectations outright, but like Watson, we've felt them and consequently lived them—leading to two of the three of us leaving the classroom for a period because trying to live all of these expectations burned us out.

The way to defang these unspoken expectations is to speak about them. As teachers of language, we know that there is great power into putting things into words—especially rarely talked-about things such as the following:

- **Be clear and consistent with our predictable time off (PTO).** Later in this chapter, we get deeper into PTO, but we encourage being clear and consistent with students and parents/guardians about when you will and won't be checking email or responding to texts. We also encourage planning your time off and even putting it into a planning calendar in the same way that one would plan the start of a unit or a final assessment.

- **Ask for the help we need.** Far too many teachers act as if they are the sole inhabitants of an island of seemingly infinite work. Of course, those teachers are not alone; they are literally surrounded by people—fellow teachers, parents, learning networks, and the students themselves. While it can contrast with the teacher-as-martyr history and mindset discussed earlier, don't be afraid to enlist the help of those around you to lighten your load. Ask that teacher down the hall about her lesson plans. Invite parents and guardians to contribute to building your classroom library. And even get the students themselves involved!

- **Bring up times when unspoken expectations impact our lives negatively.** We don't want to be the crabs in a barrel, offering an endless stream of complaints, but that doesn't mean that it isn't all right or even important to question respectfully why teachers are expected to work late or buy all the whiteboards in their classes. If done thoughtfully, and especially with others in productive conversation, improvements can result.

- **It is OK to not always be working.** If you feel strongly that the unspoken expectations around teacher workload are harmful, we encourage you to join communities like Angela Watson's 40-Hour Teacher Workweek Club (www. join.40htw.com) that discuss and explore ways to find balance and great teaching at the same time.

- **Teachers are not alone in the classroom.** We share the classroom with our students, and they can help when it comes to dismantling some of those unspoken expectations. Here are some ways to spread the work around in a way that is both better for teachers *and* the students:

  - **Have students select mentor texts.** Not all mentor texts need to or even should be chosen by the teacher. If you are studying narratives, nature poetry, or how to write strong reviews, have students bring in examples that speak to them to supplement the examples that speak to you.
  - **Crowdsource bulletin boards.** Instagram-worthy bulletin boards are lovely, but often, teachers can get just as much or more impact from having students help with decorating the room. Students can print out favorite sentences or quotes, write short book talks, or even submit proposals to paint murals. These can add meaning and community—and they don't cost a dollar or a minute for the teacher.
  - **Have students serve as "social chairs."** It's natural to want to end a text with a little celebration: get some snacks and sodas—maybe a pizza—play some music, present some projects. The only problem is that a party can end up being a lot of work for any teacher alone. Matt Kay has had success asking students to volunteer as "social chairs" to organize various activities, put together their class's potlucks, and so on.

Notes

How Can I Manage the Unspoken Expectations Placed on Teachers?

123

As a Teacher, When (and How) Should I Say No?

So here's the deal: We are finite beings with finite time. We get 24 hours per day and seven days each week, just the same as our neighbors.

Obvious, right?

But how many teachers do you know who habitually say yes to every opportunity they get offered?

- Hey, the tennis coach resigned. Want to coach tennis?

- Hey, the eighth-grade class needs a sponsor, and kids say you'd be great at it. Want me to sign you up?

- Hey, you're such a good systems thinker, and we need someone for the school improvement committee. Would you consider doing this? It'd look great on a résumé.

- Hey, we're putting in a proposal to present at a local conference in the fall. Want to be in on it?

- Hey, we need someone to start a leadership elective class next semester. I immediately thought of you. Want in?

- Hey, we're doing a book study on the latest gem from Penny Kittle and Kelly Gallagher. You're in, right?

It's classic, and it's hard to blame folks for asking us to do all this stuff. Middle and high school ELA teachers are generally pretty awesome and pretty willing to lend a hand.

But just because something is good doesn't mean we should do it. Cal Newport has a name for any decision-making process that starts out by asking whether or not something could be beneficial. He calls it the "any-benefit approach" to decision-making (2016, p. 186). The trouble with this approach is that it leads us to saying yes to . . . well, about anything. Because in a school setting, lots of things are good! Lots of things help students. Lots of things build colleague relationships. Lots of things help us broaden our careers. The question is what precious few things are you after in your work? How about in your life? Which things matter most? In this book, we offer up four reflective activities to master before extending yourself too much further:

- **Filter through your highest priority.** Dave has what he calls an Everest sentence—a sentence summarizing what he's after with his students in a given school year—hanging at the front of his classroom (see Figure 5.1). It reads, "We are all about becoming better thinkers, readers, writers, speakers, and people." Dave uses this to help him decide if he should pursue new ideas or not. For example, once he had a group of students who were really into coding, and they wanted to learn it bad. Dave had an idea: *Maybe I could* host a Coding Challenge Weekend and open my classroom one Saturday and Sunday for students to come in and complete a coding course or two. So cool, right? Except it would mean Dave was disrupting his family time for an entire weekend, and he'd be more tired on Monday, and he'd only be tangentially at best addressing his Everest. In other words, think through the benefit for students versus the cost for you and your family.

Figure 5.1 Dave's Everest Sentence poster

We are all about becoming:
- better thinkers,
- better readers,
- better writers,
- better speakers,
- and better people.

Source: Stuart - These 6 Things (2018)

- **Avoid specificity.** If someone requests something of you during your prep or after school or during the weekend, it's OK to say, "I can't make it because of scheduling conflicts." This vague (but honest) response doesn't invite the requester to try to solve a specific conflict—for example, "Oh, your wife is away that weekend and you've got all the kids? No problem! I can watch the kids while you do the thing I'm requesting!" (Newport, 2016, p. 239).

- **Refrain from consolation prizes.** Let's say a student comes up to you and says, "Hey, I wrote a 50,000-word fan-fiction novel, and I'm going to get it published. Can you edit it for me?" Dave used to respond to questions like this with something like, "You know, professional writers don't have their teachers do their editing for them, so I don't want to start you off on a bad habit. But I'd be happy to read it!" That last is the consolation prize because you're still putting in the time but the student isn't gaining anything either. Cal Newport puts it this way in *Deep Work* (2016): "A clean break is best."

- **Pause awkwardly.** If someone makes a request of you in person, you might feel compelled to answer quickly with an unconsidered "yes." One way to avoid this is to just pause. It might be awkward, but it gives you a minute to think—and it might even give your requester a minute to give you an out (this one is from Greg McKeown's *Essentialism*, 2014). It is also all right to extend that pause further to think on it and collect your thoughts, although don't let it hang too long, as that can cause anxiety for you and the person who made the request.

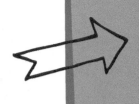

How Can I Stay a Writer While Teaching Writing? How About a Reader While Teaching Reading?

We became ELA teachers because we love young people and we love language. And we want students to love books. We want them to find joy and purpose in expressing themselves through writing. It's easy, however, for us to lose a bit of our own passion for reading and writing as we try to foster it in our students. This is not unlike elite dancers who feel their zeal for dance fade because of constant pressure to nail the next show.

The more our personal reading and writing lives take a back seat, the more inauthentic our passion for language might seem to our students. (Not to mention the less likely it will be for us to randomly think of cool supplementary sources from our personal reading at just the right moment.) Perhaps more importantly, the more disconnected we are from the literary passions that brought us to this moment, the less happy we might be. Life's too short for that.

Here are some ways that we can maintain our own passion for reading and writing even while grinding through our first years teaching:

- **Be OK with adjusting your reading habits to your new level of busyness.** Don't fight it. Matt Kay, for instance, is all about the audiobooks during the commute to school. Meanwhile, Dave Stuart is fine with starting and stopping books as he sees fit—a chapter from this one during breakfast, a snippet from a different one during lunch, the intro to a third one while he falls asleep in bed. The idea of "finishing books" just isn't something Dave stresses about—at all—because he reads to learn, not to perform.

- **Start a book club with students and/or colleagues!** This can happen online, with discussion boards, or with a biweekly meeting. Sometimes, all we need is the added layer of gentle accountability and community.

- **Regularly do the prompts and even the creative projects you give students.** During the five minutes students are writing on a prompt, we can be tempted to grade a paper or two, take attendance, or glance at our email. In those little snippets of time, it might be worth trying to stay in the moment to take creative advantage of your own thoughtful prompting. Further, when you first assign a cool creative project, take a crack at it. Not only will modeling it help build camaraderie with your students, but you also might also end up with something that turns into *something*! You could, of course, do only a part of the project (whatever you have time for).

- **Read fewer professional books and more books just for fun.** Dave Stuart had his biggest breakthroughs as a teacher when he stopped reading new PD books and kept reading the same one over and over again for an entire straight school year (it was Mike Schmoker's *Focus* [2011]). In addition to the sanity-boosting nature of having less stuff that you "have to" read, this strategy makes it possible to pick up more books just for fun. Did your neighbor recommend a Winston Churchill bio that sounds cool? Pick it up. Don't like it? Put it down. Is one of your high school students reading a graphic novel that sounds sweet? Get yourself a copy from the library. Read it for pleasure. Sometimes, we teachers can turn reading into a big time grind, but it doesn't have to be!

- **Seek out seemingly unrelated things when feeling stuck.** Matt Johnson regularly picks up a philosophy/sci-fi/fantasy book or writes bad poetry or ranty op-eds that no one else sees (or should see) when his reading/writing tanks run low. The brain is a glorious connection-making machine, and the connections that arise when reading and writing disparate things can often unlock exciting ideas and paths forward.

Notes

How Can I Stay a Writer While Teaching Writing? How About a Reader While Teaching Reading?

127

CAREER

How Can Professional Learning and Professional Communities Keep You Excited About Teaching—and Help You Work Faster and Better?

All three of us are parents and teachers in public school classrooms with lots of students, yet we are also all members of professional learning groups, ranging from large national organizations such as the National Writing Project (NWP) and National Council of Teachers of English (NCTE) to small-scale book clubs and personal professional learning networks.

On the surface, this might seem like we are work gluttons who can't help but to continually overload our plates with all things education. And although we, like most, can at times take on too much, the reason we engage with these professional learning groups is precisely because we want to be both quality teachers and quality parents, partners, friends, and family.

That balance is difficult, but it is best achieved for us when we work toward it with other teachers across our schools, districts, counties, and countries. If not for the mentors he met in the NWP, for example, Matt Johnson would have never realized that his overcorrecting and overediting of student papers were unnecessary—a drain on his time that wasn't leading to more student learning (see Chapter 3 for solutions to this challenge). For Dave Stuart, paying attention to the colleagues students describe as "good teachers" has led to insights into deep principles of teaching. Seeing someone with an entirely different style from him accomplish an effective writing lesson is super informative for Dave, and he loves the friendships that have developed from seeking out folks who do and think about things differently than he does. Similarly, Matt Kay's practice has grown because of relationships formed with the fellow coaches in his slam poetry league. He has picked up all manner of prompts and activities from them and has learned better ways to keep creative writing fresh for his students.

These gains—the reclamation of dozens or even hundreds of hours a year for Matt J., the inspiration that helped fuel Dave's growth as a teacher, or the fresh set of activities suggested from fellow writing and performance coaches for Matt K.— more than made up for the initial time and effort expended, and they are only three examples. The number of better and faster practices that we've learned from our colleagues over the years is one of the main reasons we have the space to write these words right here. Further, the sense of meaning, energy, camaraderie, and mentorship that one can find in finding the right group can sharpen and focus us during the hours we do work.

Matt Johnson is a longtime runner, and one of the things that has always struck him about distance running is how one could easily guess that it would be a drain on one's energy, but in reality, it is anything but. While a particularly long or hard run can make one temporarily gulp for air, over the long term, those long and hard runs make one sharper and more energetic. The same is true for reaching out to those teachers out there with you. The initial energy and time needed might seem like one more thing in a day that doesn't need any more things, but once one does connect with the right teachers, the energy and time saved over the long term can make the initial reaching-out one of the best returns on investment one can make.

Great Resources

Check out these professional learning communities (PLCs):

- ERWC—Expository Reading and Writing Course, the California State University (www.writing.csusuccess.org)

- Penny Kittle's Book Love Foundation Summer Book Club (www.booklovefoundation.org)

- National Council of Teachers of English (www.ncte.org)

- National Writing Project (www.nwp.org)

Notes

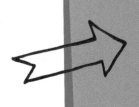

I'm Bringing Home Work on Nights and Weekends, and It's Driving Me/My Friends/ My Partner Crazy. What Can I Do?

All right, embarrassing story time. Early in his teaching career, Dave Stuart had a moment where he was talking to a romantic interest on the phone one night and telling her how many hours he worked. "Sometimes," Dave said in a husky tone, "the only way I see the sun shine is through my classroom window. When I show up to school, it's dark. And when I leave school, it's dark."

Dave's conversation partner was not impressed. She immediately responded, "That is one of the dumbest things I've ever heard. How do you even know if what you're working on actually works?" Dave got two great things out of this conversation:

1. A lifelong relationship (he's now married to this mythically insightful person)
2. A deep insight into work

What's that deep insight? Today, most people call it Parkinson's Law, after the author who first described the concept in a mid-twentieth century article in *The Economist* (Parkinson, 1955). Here it is:

 Work expands to fill the time that you give it.

It's such an important concept for folks who work a job like teaching because teaching is one of those jobs with both crazy complexity and a built-in sense of purpose. If we give 90 hours per week to teaching, guess what? We'll find work to fill each one of those hours. But if we give only 50 hours per week to teaching, guess what? We've got to work pretty hard at figuring out which work matters the most, and this accelerates the improvement of our impact as teachers.

To constrain your working hours, try these things:

● **Make some predictable time off (PTO) goals and share them with a group of friends or colleagues who have similar goals.** Years ago, researcher Leslie Perlow (2012) predicted that predictable time off could enhance performance in elite professional settings. To test this, she and her co-researcher Jessica Porter worked with a team at one of the world's most elite and demanding professional consulting firms—we're talking about a company where clients were used to 24/7 access to their consultants (sound like any parents/guardians or students you've worked with?) and where 80-hour weeks were the norm for teammates (know any teachers putting in about that much?)—and they simply requested that everyone on the team go through a simple process:

  ● Team members agreed upon a unit of predictable time off and made this their goal each week.
  ● The team met each week to discuss progress toward their PTO goals.

As it turned out, Perlow and Porter were right: This simple process improved work performance for study participants. Try something like this in your own setting with colleagues who have similar goals as you.

- **Set a work schedule for yourself.** One common cause of work time bloat is when we lack clarity about what it is that we're trying to accomplish. For example, after the final bell rings and students head their various ways for the day, teachers commonly experience their worst productivity hours. Sitting aimlessly at a computer with a stack of papers to read, emails to respond to, and lessons to plan, we can end up drowning in the algorithmic vortexes of YouTube or Twitter. Instead, set goal-oriented time blocks in your working hours—for example, "During the first half of my prep, I'm going to read 15 student essays; during the second half, I'm going to process my emails for the day."

- **Speaking of email: Check it as infrequently as you can, and only handle it once (OHIO).** Email is the perfect productivity killer. It feels as if you're doing something productive when you check it, but on the scale of teacher work most likely to positively impact student long-term flourishing, email tends to be pretty inconsequential. A sane approach to email can look like this:

  - Check it one or two times per day at predetermined times.
  - When you check, "OHIO": only handle it once. With this term, we mean that every email becomes replied to (e.g., quick question emails), turned into a task (e.g., emails that require thinking or research), read and archived (e.g., newsletter emails), or archived without even being read (e.g., newsletter emails that you don't have time to read this week or blast emails from your colleagues that don't apply to you).

- **Don't multitask work and relaxation.** Remember that article "Why Multitasking Is a Myth That's Breaking Your Brain and Wasting Your Time" from Chapter 4? Humans can't actually multitask, so when we try to multitask work and relaxation, we don't do either particularly well, and we lose a ton of time. So when bingeing the new season of your favorite show, binge that show. When planning a lesson, plan a lesson. Your students, you, and the people in your life will all be glad you did!

Notes

How Can I Avoid Burnout?

In order to avoid burnout, it helps to understand where it comes from. Some folks might gain this understanding through something like the World Health Organization's definition of occupational burnout:

> Burnout is a syndrome conceptualized as resulting from chronic workplace stress that has not been successfully managed. It is characterized by three dimensions:

- feelings of energy depletion or exhaustion;
- increased mental distance from one's job, or feelings of negativism or cynicism related to one's job; and
- reduced professional efficacy. (2019, paras. 4–6)

Others might like something a bit more conceptual like the Workload-Pressure Whirlpool, shown in Figure 5.2.

Figure 5.2 The Workload-Pressure Whirlpool

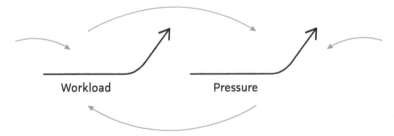

As workload goes up, pressure goes up. As pressure goes up, our ability to effectively manage our workload decreases . . . so our workload goes up.

Then, *teaching* happens, meaning you get daily external doses of added workload and added pressure.

It's a whirlpool.

There are two basic strategies for getting out of the whirlpool:

1. Get good at depressurization.
2. Get good at "deworkloadification."

For depressurization, we recommend these steps:

- **Remind yourself that you're not you're job.** When your sense of self is tied to your performance as a teacher, your life becomes a pressure cooker. Toni Morrison (2017) wrote an amazing essay in which she recalls complaining to her dad about work, and her dad tells her something along the lines of, "That's your job, not your life." From his comment, she took away the following:

  1. Whatever the work is, do it well—not for the boss, but for yourself.
  2. You make the job; it doesn't make you.
  3. Your real life is with your family.
  4. You are not the work you do; you are the person you are.

  For Morrison, these realizations were a breakthrough that carried her through all kinds of jobs.

- **Take a five-out, five-in.** At the points in your school day where you're about toast, set a timer for five minutes and walk away from your (studentless) classroom toward the "naturey-est" place you can reach. Maybe it's a pair of trees by the sidewalk; maybe it's a park; maybe it's a field. When the timer goes off, walk back. During the entire 10 minutes, no noise, no inputs, no productivity. Just walk, breathe, think, pray, reflect. Depressurize.

- **Go to bed.** It turns out that a lot of us view 10 p.m. and after as the time to exert our autonomy (Singh, 2021). We stay up later than we want to, and then we're exhausted the next day, which we fix with large doses of the world's most widely consumed solution to tiredness (ahhh, coffee). Better idea? Go to bed on time.

- **Having some hard emotions about work?** It turns out that persistent emotions such as anger, fear, bitterness, and jealousy don't go away by complaining with friends. If you're experiencing these, take heart. It's way more normal than it feels. But also? Take action. Ask friends and colleagues you trust if there are mental health resources that might be within your budget or job benefits package. Short of that, try taking some time in solitude to examine these emotions via journaling. The QR code in the margin takes you to a self-examination protocol Dave recommends for starting to get to the root of difficult feelings.

Self-examination protocol

For workload simplification, consider these solutions:

- **Satisfice work that doesn't matter most.** When asked this question, what are the first tasks that come to mind: What's the most pointless thing that you do daily in your job? Whatever your answer is, chances are that it's a thing that can be satisficed, or done at the bare-minimum threshold of acceptability rather than any kind of optimized or maximized threshold. This idea of satisficing comes from a Nobel Prize–winning economist named Herbert Simon, but you and I need to claim this idea for teaching. There isn't a way to do the work of a teacher in the twenty-first century without being very picky about what we optimize and what we satisfice. You can't answer every email optimally, plus give feedback on every assignment optimally, plus engage with the greater school community optimally, plus join every committee. Things have to give. We have to choose.

- **Sometimes, tasks can be skipped altogether.** Many teachers, out of an abundance of conscientiousness, add tasks to their plates that can double or triple their workload. If you have unlimited hours in which to do your work and superhuman-level endurance, then this might not be a bad way to go. But 99 percent of us mortals can't maintain that kind of thing. So we need to regularly ask ourselves these questions when we become overloaded with tasks:

    a. What am I after in my job? What's my top aim for students in this course or unit or lesson or day?
    b. Which of the tasks that are currently overloading my list are furthest removed from that goal?
    c. Which of these tasks might no one notice if I skipped them?

- **Set constraints.** Self-imposed constraints are a major secret to fast-forwarding your path to insights about the work that matters most in teaching. Set a work schedule and stick to it. When you tell yourself that you only get x hours to work this week, and when you're clear with yourself when exactly these hours take place, it reframes your thinking about your workload. You stop saying, "When can I get this all done," and you start having to say, "Wait, I don't have enough time to get all of this done." So which of these things on my list matter the most? Which can be satisficed or skipped?

Notes

What's the Best Way to Get Better as a Teacher?

In our experience, there are many paths to growing in your expertise as a teacher, but they are not all equally fruitful. In the following paragraphs, you'll find a tip or two from each of us that has mattered the most in accelerating our growth in the profession. We've left a few blank boxes for you, and for these, we recommend that you go to colleagues you respect and ask them what they believe is the best way to get better as a teacher.

- **Seek the counsel of an in-person mentor.** One of Dave Stuart's favorite methods for improving is making note of any time that a student makes a genuine remark about the quality of another teacher. At any point he heard something like this, especially early in his career, he'd go out of his way to ask the teacher if he might sit in on a class during his prep hour, just to watch. Whenever Dave saw something that he didn't understand but that seemed excellent (e.g., his colleague Doug's use of exemplars in writing instruction; his colleague Frazier's ability to help learners cultivate reading identities), he'd hang around after class and ask a specific question about the thing he observed so that he could experiment with what he learned and then come back to the colleague and report on what he learned. What Dave found is that this simple behavior didn't just help him greatly in his classroom; it also helped him to build rapport with a wide range of colleagues who were well loved by students.

- **Seek the counsel of a distant mentor.** Another of our tricks is that when a teacher author catches our attention (e.g., Penny Kittle, Jim Burke, Carol Jago, Pedro Noguera, Kelly Gallagher, Cornelius Minor, Linda Christensen, etc.), we set aside several months of reading time to only read what the person of interest has published. We do our best during these "research sprints" to get to the bottom of basic questions: How does this person approach teaching? How would this person handle X or Y obstacle that I'm experiencing in my class right now? By giving focused reading to single teacher–authors, we eventually find that we gain a sense of understanding how the focal teacher thinks about key issues in the classroom, and this allows us to call upon the mentor at any time that we think they can help.

- **Be a digital packrat.** Years ago, Matt Kay learned how important it was to not only keep all of his old unit plans and assignment sheets but also to download all of the student work at the end of the year and keep it in a folder. It can be arranged any way that makes sense for you. Matt puts all old student work in one folder, separated by year. He puts all old assignment sheets, unit plans, and the like in other folders. This helps in many ways. First, we don't have to start from scratch when we decide to bring back a gem from yesteryear. This frees up a lot of time to either polish them or work on other things. Second, we have plenty of student mentor texts at the ready for projects that we've done before. Third, we have plenty of actual content to reflect upon and can track where we have gotten better over time.

CAREER

● **Make time for meaningful reflection.** We are admittedly biased, but we find teaching to be one of the most complex and ever-evolving professions there is. To steward 30 or 35 students per class period toward deep understanding of often tricky topics, to help them cultivate their own internal beliefs, and to manage the interpersonal dynamics of a room filled with young people is challenging to say the least—and rewarding. It also is ever-evolving, with each new group of students and each new year bringing myriad challenges. When it comes to managing these shifting challenges, we have found a through line in our practices and in the practices of the great teachers we've known to be regular meaningful reflection. This reflection comes in many forms—from blogging and journaling about what happened in class to composing poetry or tweets that capture the moments of the day—but the key, like a swimmer paddling in the middle of a river, is to keep evolving as the current shifts, twists, and turns with each new moment.

Notes

REFERENCES

Agarwal, P. K., & Bain, P. M. (2019). *Powerful teaching: Unleashing the science of learning*. Jossey-Bass.

Allington, R. L. (2002). What I've learned about effective reading instruction: From a decade of studying exemplary elementary classroom teachers. *Phi Delta Kappan, 83*, 740–747. https://doi.org/10.1177/003172170208301007.

Allington, R. L. (2014). How reading volume affects both reading fluency and reading achievement. *International Electronic Journal of Elementary Education, 7*(1), 13–26. https://files.eric.ed.gov/fulltext/EJ1053794.pdf.

Ambady, N., Shih, M., Kim, A., & Pittinsky, T. L. (2001). Deflecting negative self-relevant stereotype activation: The effects of individuation. *Journal of Experimental Social Psychology, 40*, 401–408.

Anthony, A. (2021). David Eagleman: "The working of the brain resembles drug dealers in Albuquerque." *The Guardian*. https://www.theguardian.com/science/2021/jun/12/david-eagleman-the-working-of-the-brain-resembles-drug-dealers-in-albuquerque.

Aronson, J., Lustina, M. J., Good, C., Keough, K., Steele, C. M., & Brown, J. (1999). When white men can't do math: Necessary and sufficient factors in stereotype threat. *Journal of Experimental Social Psychology, 35*, 29–46.

Baumrind, D. (1966). Effects of authoritative parental control on child behavior. *Child Development, 37*(4), 887–907.

Belanger, J., & Allingham, P. V. (2004). *Using "think aloud" methods to investigate the processes secondary school students use to respond to their teachers' comments on their written work* [Technical report]. University of British Columbia.

Blackwelder, A. (2020). Going gradeless and doing the "actual work." In S. Blum (Ed.), *Ungrading: Why rating students undermines learning (and what to do instead)*. West Virginia University Press.

Calderon, V., & Yu, D. (2017). Student enthusiasm falls as high school graduation nears. *Gallup*. https://news.gallup.com/opinion/gallup/211631/student-enthusiasm-falls-high-school-graduation-nears.aspx.

Castillo, M. (2013, July 4). *Reading, writing may help preserve memory in older age*. CBS News. https://www.cbsnews.com/news/reading-writing-may-help-preserve-memory-in-older-age/.

Chanock, K. (2000). Comments on essays: Do students understand what tutors write? *Teaching in Higher Education, 5*(1), 96–105.

Cho, Y. H., & Cho, K. (2011). Peer reviewers learn from giving comments. *Instructional Science, 39*(5), 629–643. https//doi.org/10.1007/s11251-010-9146-1.

Christensen, L. (2009). *Teaching for joy and justice*. Rethinking Schools.

Cook, C. R., Fiat, A., & Larson, M. (2018). Positive greetings at the door: Evaluation of a low-cost, high-yield proactive classroom management strategy. *Journal of Positive Behavior Interventions, 20*(3). https://journals.sagepub.com/doi/10.1177/1098300717753831.

Costa, A. L., & Kallick, B. (2008). Learning through reflection. In A. L. Costa, & B. Kallick (Eds.), *Learning and leaning with habits of mind: 16 essential characteristics for success* (pp. 221–235). ASCD. http://www.ascd.org/publications/books/108008/chapters/Learning-Through-Reflection.aspx.

Crisp, B. (2007). Is it worth the effort? How feedback influences students' subsequent submission of assessable work. *Assessment and Evaluation in Higher Education, 32*(5), 571–581. https://doi.org/10.1080/02602930601116912.

Damon, W. (2009). *The path to purpose: How young people find their calling in life*. Free Press.

Disney Institute Blog. (2018, February 7). *Exceeding guest expectations: Go beyond the obvious*. https://www.disneyinstitute.com/blog/exceeding-guest-expectations-go-beyond-the-obvious/.

Doolittle, P. (2013, November). *Peter Doolittle: How your "working memory" makes sense of the world* [Video]. YouTube. https://www.youtube.com/watch?v=UWKvpFZJwcE.

Duckworth, A. L., Kirby, T., Gollwitzer, A., & Oettingen, G. (2013). From fantasy to action: Mental contrasting with implementation intentions (MCII) improves academic performance in children. *Social Psychological and Personality Science, 4*(6), 745–753. https://doi.org/10.1177/1948550613476307.

Earl E. Bakken Center for Spirituality and Healing. (n.d.). Reading for stress relief. *University of Minnesota*. https://www.takingcharge.csh.umn.edu/reading-stress-relief.

Education Alliance. (n.d.). *Culturally responsive teaching*. Brown University. https://www.brown.edu/academics/education-alliance/teaching-diverse-learners/strategies-0/culturally-responsive-teaching-0#ladson-billings

eMediaMillWorks. (2000, July 10). Text: George W. Bush's speech to the NAACP. *Washington Post.com*. https://www.washingtonpost.com/wp-srv/onpolitics/elections/bushtext071000.htm.

Feldman, J. (2019). *Grading for equity: What it is, why it matters, and how it can transform schools and classrooms*. Corwin.

Fisher, D., & Frey, N. (2018). Show & tell: A video column—Teachers as early warning detectors. *Mental Health in Schools, 75*(4), 80–81.

Fisher, D., Frey, N., Quaglia, R., Smith, D., & Lande, L. (2018). *Engagement by design: Creating learning environments where students thrive*. Corwin.

Fletcher, J. (2021). *Writing rhetorically: Fostering responsive thinkers and communicators*. Stenhouse.

Flood, A. (2016, August 8). Book up for a longer life: Readers die later, study finds. *The Guardian*. https://www.theguardian.com/books/2016/aug/08/book-up-for-a-longer-life-readers-die-later-study-finds.

Fotuhi, O. (2020, October 21). The need to combat a false growth mind-set. *Inside Higher Ed*. https://www.insidehighered.com/views/2020/10/21/misperceptions-among-professors-about-growth-mind-set-concept-may-be-harming-some.

Fuller, D. (1987). Teacher commentary that communicates: Practicing what we preach in the writing class. *Journal of Teaching Writing, 6*(2), 307–317. https//doi.org/10.1177/1050651907300466.

Gallagher, K. (2009). *Readicide: How schools are killing reading and what you can do about it*. Stenhouse.

Goodreads. (n.d.a). *James Baldwin quotes*. https://www.goodreads.com/quotes/5853-you-think-your-pain-and-your-heartbreak-are-unprecedented-in.

Goodreads. (n.d.b). *Maya Angelou quotes*. https://www.goodreads.com/quotes/1035-when-i-look-back-i-am-so-impressed-again-with.

Hammond, C. (2019). Does reading fiction make us better people? *BBC*. https://www.bbc.com/future/article/20190523-does-reading-fiction-make-us-better-people.

Hammond, Z. (2014). *Culturally responsive teaching and the brain*. Corwin.

Hart-Davidson, B. (2014). *Describe—evaluate—success: Giving helpful feedback, with Bill Hart-Davidson* [Video]. https://elireview.com/2016/08/03/describe-evaluate-suggest/.

Hattie, J. (2012). *Visible learning for teachers: Maximizing impact on learning*. Routledge.

Hattie, J., & Clarke, S. (2019). *Visible learning feedback*. Corwin.

Hicks, T., & Schoenborn, A. (2020). *Creating confident writers: For high school, college, and life*. Norton.

Hulleman, C. S., & Harackiewicz, J. M. (2009). Promoting interest and performance in high school science classes. *Science, 326*, 1410–1412.

Ice, P., Curtis, R., Phillips, P., & Wells, J. (2007). Using asynchronous audio feedback to enhance teaching presence and students' sense of community. *Journal of Asynchronous Learning Networks, 11*(2). https//doi.org/11.10.24059/olj.v11i2.1724.

John, A. (2013, July 8). More scientific evidence that reading is good for you. *The Atlantic*. https://www.theatlantic.com/national/archive/2013/07/more-evidence-reading-good-you/313575/.

Khan, M. (2020, October 25). Survey: Students' feelings about high school are not positive. *Inter Press Service News Agency*. https://ipsnews.net/business/2020/10/25/survey-students-feelings-about-high-school-are-not-positive/.

Kleinfeld, J. (1975). Effective teachers of Eskimo and Indian students. *School Review, 83*(2), 301–344. https://www.jstor.org/stable/1084645.

Laymon, K. (2015, November 19). Da art of storytellin' (a prequel). *Oxford American: A Magazine of the South, 91*(Winter). https://main.oxfordamerican.org/magazine/item/702-da-art-of-storytellin.

Mascle, D. (2016, March 29). 7 strategies to improve conferences with writers. *Metawriting*. https://metawriting.deannamascle.com/7-strategies-improve-conferences-writers/.

Mason, C. (2017). *Home education*. Living Book Press.

McChesney, C., Covey, S., & Juling, J. (2012). *The 4 disciplines of execution: Achieving your wildly important goals*. Simon & Schuster.

McKeown, G. (2014). *Essentialism: The disciplined pursuit of less*. Crown Business.

Merrill, S. (2020, September 11). Trauma is "written into our bodies"—but educators can help. *Edutopia*. https://www.edutopia.org/article/trauma-written-our-bodies-educators-can-help.

Minor, C. (2018). *We got this: Equity access, and the quest to be who our students need us to be*. Heinemann.

Morrison, T. (2017, May 29). The work you do, the person you are. *New Yorker*. https://www.newyorker.com/magazine/2017/06/05/the-work-you-do-the-person-you-are.

National Center for Education Statistics. (2012). *The nation's report card: Writing 2011* (NCES 2012–470). Institute of Education Sciences, U.S. Department of Education. https://nces.ed.gov/nationsreportcard/pdf/main2011/2012470.pdf.

National Commission on Writing for America's Families, Schools, and Colleges. (2004). *Writing: A ticket to work... or a ticket out.* College Entrance Examination Board.

National Council of Teachers of English. (2019, November 7). *Statement on independent reading.* https://ncte.org/statement/independent-reading/.

Newkirk, T. (2017). *Embarrassment: And the emotional underlife of learning.* Heinemann.

Newkirk, T. (2021). *Writing unbound: How fiction transforms student writers.* Heinemann.

Newport, C. (2016). *Deep work: Rules for focused success in a distracted world.* Hachette Book Group.

Nguyen, H. (2021, May 17). How to provide less structure for independent reading. *Edutopia.* https://www.edutopia.org/article/how-provide-less-structure-independent-reading.

Parkinson, C. N. (1955, November 19). Parkinson's Law. *Economist.* https://www.economist.com/news/1955/11/19/parkinsons-law.

Perlow, L. (2012). *Sleeping with your smartphone: How to break the 24/7 habit and change the way you work.* Harvard Business School.

Purdie, N., & Hattie, J. (2002). Assessing students' conceptions of learning. *Australian Journal of Educational & Developmental Psychology, 2,* 17–32.

Reading & Writing Project: Teachers College Columbia University. (n.d.). *Research base underlying the Teachers College Reading and Writing Workshop's approach to literacy instruction.* https://members.readingandwritingproject.org/about/research-base.

Rice, P. C. (2017, November 15). *Pronouncing students' names correctly should be a big deal.* EducationWeek. https://www.edweek.org/leadership/opinion-pronouncing-students-names-correctly-should-be-a-big-deal/2017/11.

Richards, B. A., & Frankland, P. W. (2017). The persistence and transience of memory. *Neuron, 94,* 1071–1084. cell.com/neuron/fulltext/S0896-6273(17)30365–3.

Rousell, M. (2021). *The power of surprise: How your brain secretly changes your beliefs.* Rowman & Littlefield.

Schmoker, M. (2011). *Focus: Elevating the essentials to radically improve student learning.* ASCD.

Sims-Bishop, R. (1990). Mirrors, windows, and sliding glass doors. *Perspectives: Choosing and Using Books for the Classroom, 6*(3).

Singh, A. (2021, June 23). What's revenge bedtime procrastination and how do I stop it? *The Cut.* https://www.thecut.com/article/how-to-stop-revenge-bedtime-procrastination.html.

Stateside Staff. (2017). *Exhibit brings high school students from Lansing, Flint together to depict life without safe water.* Michigan Radio. https://www.michiganradio.org/families-community/2017–01-27/exhibit-brings-high-school-students-from-lansing-flint-together-to-depict-life-without-safe-water.

Steele, C. M., & Aronson, J. (1995). Stereotype threat and the intellectual test performance of African American students. *Journal of Personality and Social Psychology, 69,* 797–811.

Stuart, D., Jr. (2018). *These 6 things: How to focus your teaching on what matters most.* Corwin.

Thompson, M. E. (n.d.). *TQE: Thoughts, questions, and epiphanies.* https://www.unlimitedteacher.com/tqe.

Toren, M. (2017, September 28). Why multitasking is a myth that's breaking your brain and wasting your time. *Entrepreneur.* https://www.entrepreneur.com/article/299029.

Tsai, E. (2019, March 6). Teaching great writing one sentence at a time. *New York Times.* https://www.nytimes.com/2019/03/06/learning/teaching-great-writing-one-sentence-at-a-time.html.

Watson, A. (2019). *Fewer things, better: The courage to focus on what matters most.* Due Season Press.

Wiggins, G., & McTighe, J. (2005). *Understanding by design* (2nd ed.). ASCD.

Wiliam, D. (2018, September 17). *Strategy 3: Providing feedback that moves learning forward* [Video]. YouTube. https://www.youtube.com/watch?v=vdlk9ysWJXQ.

Willingham, D. T. (2007, Summer). Critical thinking: Why is it so hard to teach? *American Educator,* 8–19. http://www.aft.org/sites/default/files/periodicals/Crit_Thinking.pdf.

Wlodkowski, R. J. (1983). *Motivational opportunities for successful teaching* [leader's guide]. Universal Dimensions.

World Health Organization. (2019, May 28). Burnout an "occupational phenomenon": International classification of diseases. *Departmental News.* https://www.who.int/news/item/28–05–2019-burn-out-an-occupational-phenomenon-international-classification-of-diseases.

Zerwin, S. (2020). *Point/Less: An English teacher's guide to more meaningful grading.* Heinemann.

Zimmerman, J., & Robertson, E. (2017). *The case for contention: Teaching controversial issues in American schools.* University of Chicago Press.

INDEX

Answers to Your Biggest Questions About Teaching Middle and High School ELA

Because...
ALL TEACHERS ARE LEADERS

DOMINIQUE SMITH, DOUGLAS FISHER, NANCY FREY
Take an active approach toward disrupting the negative effects of labels and assumptions that interfere with student learning.

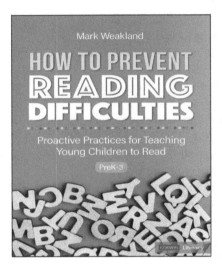

MARK WEAKLAND
Build on decades of evidence and years of experience to understand how the brain learns to read and how to apply that understanding to Tier 1 instruction.

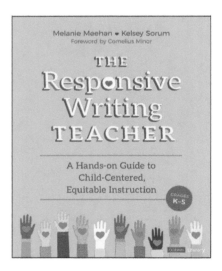

MELANIE MEEHAN, KELSEY SORUM
Learn how to adapt curriculum to meet the needs of the whole child. Each chapter offers intentional steps for responsive instruction across four domains: academic, linguistic, cultural, and social-emotional.

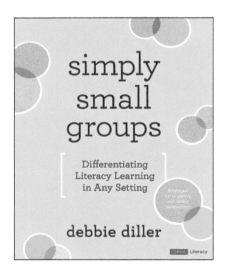

DEBBIE DILLER
Discover concrete guidance for tailoring the small-group experience to literacy instruction in order to give every reader a pathway to success.

To order your copies, visit **corwin.com/literacy**

At Corwin Literacy we have put together a collection of just-in-time, classroom-tested, practical resources from trusted experts that allow you to quickly find the information you need when you need it.

DOUGLAS FISHER, NANCY FREY, NICOLE LAW

Using a structured, three-pronged approach—skill, will, and thrill—students experience reading as a purposeful act with this new comprehensive model of reading instruction.

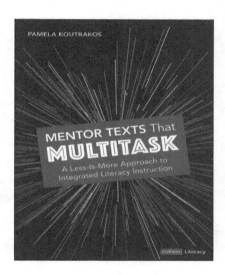

PAM KOUTRAKOS

Packed with ready-to-go lessons and tools, this user-friendly resource provides ways to weave together different aspects of literacy using one mentor text.

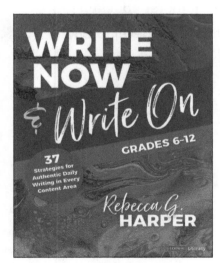

REBECCA G. HARPER

Customizable strategies turn students' informal writing into a springboard for daily writing practice in every content area—with a focus on academic vocabulary, summarizing, and using textual evidence.

MELANIE MEEHAN, CHRISTINA NOSEK, MATTHEW JOHNSON, DAVE STUART JR., MATTHEW R. KAY

This series offers actionable answers to your most pressing questions about teaching reading, writing, and ELA.

CORWIN
A SAGE Publishing Company

Helping educators make the greatest impact

CORWIN HAS ONE MISSION: to enhance education through intentional professional learning.

We build long-term relationships with our authors, educators, clients, and associations who partner with us to develop and continuously improve the best evidence-based practices that establish and support lifelong learning.